Praise for earlier editions of *The Overnight Resume*

"It's a new approach . . . teaches you to think about the employer . . . tells you exactly what to do and why. It's the style I use myself."

> —**John Noble**, associate director, Career Services, Harvard University

"Beautifully written, quite a joy to read. Walks you right through the nuts and bolts of constructing a resume."

> —**Virginia Mak**, career counselor, Stanford University

The best resume book I've seen, because of its clear and concise style. And it provides a step-by-step plan to find the right job, not just a job. A real-world approach."

> —**Teri L. Bellamy**, vice president, Human Resources, Bank of America

"Mr. Asher is expert in emphasizing strengths and camouflaging weaknesses while avoiding the potentially career-killing lie."

> —*Dallas News*

"An overnight sensation . . . you'll have a winning resume before sunup."

> —*Working Writers*

"Packed with original tips from a pro. We've seen dozens of books on the subject, and this one really stands out in a crowd."

> —**Kennedy Publications'** *Job & Career Library*

"Asher offers brevity, clear thinking, and good sense . . . His resume for Ernie the alley cat is proof positive that a resume can be created from virtually any background. Highly recommended."

> —*Library Journal*

"The most practical, readable, and down-to-earth approach to writing resumes I've ever seen . . . In my opinion, Donald Asher is among the very best in the industry. I think I've read everything he's written."

> —**Anne Follis**, author of *Power Pack Your Job Search*

The Overnight Resume

THE FASTEST WAY TO YOUR NEXT JOB

THIRD EDITION

DONALD ASHER

TEN SPEED PRESS
Berkeley

To my wife, Lisa

Published in the United States by Ten Speed Press, an imprint of the Crown Publishing
Group, a division of Random House, Inc., New York.
www.crownpublishing.com
www.tenspeed.com

Ten Speed Press and the Ten Speed Press colophon are registered trademarks of Random
House, Inc.

Library of Congress Cataloging-in-Publication Data
Asher, Donald.
 The overnight resume : the fastest way to your next job / Donald Asher. — 3rd ed.
  p. cm.
 Includes index.
 1. Resumes (Employment) I. Title.
 HF5383.A84 2010
 650.14'2—dc22

                              2009038118

ISBN 978-1-58008-091-0

Printed in the United States

Cover and interior text design by Chris Hall/Ampersand Communications

10 9 8 7 6 5 4 3 2 1

Third Edition

Acknowledgments

To my clients, who taught me all the best tricks.

To my staff: Kathy Priola, Kathleen Docherty, Penelope Bell, Kathleen Docherty, Robin Klayman, Patricia O'Keefe, Christine Lee, Kimberly Brown, Joe Caffall, Lisa Lenker, Susan Hall, Rich Matheson, Frank Antonelli, Michelle Frame, Jim Targonski, Leigh Hancock, Andrea Miskow, Marsha Keeffer, Sharon McNally, Dave Soss, David Glober, Tia Woodward, John Heed. Nobody ever had a better staff.

To Ten Speed Press: Thank you for twenty years of successful partnership. It has been a rare privilege to concentrate on writing and content, and let the true professionals handle the difficult part of ten books in multiple releases. Ten Speed Press is a real author's publisher. Special thanks to Phil, George, Sal, Mariah, Kirsty, Lorena, and most especially, Veronica.

Special thanks to the career centers at Swarthmore College, Reed College, Louisiana State University, Krannert School of Management at Purdue University, and the University of San Francisco.

The only significant difference between people who do things and people who don't is exactly that. Pick up this book and do something to make your life better.

—Donald Asher

Contents

How to Use This Book

Choose a job you love, and you will never have to work a day in your life.

—Confucius

If you want to have your resume ready by 9 A.M. tomorrow, skip the rest of this preface, and get started right now. Do **not** skip chapter 3, "The Rules of Resume Writing."

The book makes several assumptions about you, the reader. In order to best evaluate whether the book can be of use to you, you need to know what they are:

- You know what you want to do.

- You are intelligent.

- You can write a reasonable, straightforward sentence.

- You are motivated to create your own success.

What is *not* assumed:

- You are a writer or a grammarian.

This book assumes that you do not need psychoanalysis or aptitude testing; what you do need is a resume, and you need it fast. The problem with many of the books in the get-a-job genre is that they attempt to tell you how to discern what you want to do. The result is often a bit like swimming through quicksand, especially for the majority of us who know what it is we are after.

You may have picked up this book because a headhunter called you this afternoon or your favorite project got canceled or your boss yelled at you or because you just completed your doctorate in microbiology, but let us assume that what you need most is a resume and a rational job-search strategy.

My experience is that most jobseekers are employed, do not have a week to read get-a-job books, and *do* know what their immediate objective is. If you are unsure, there are many good books on the subject, but this is not one of them.

You must know what you want to do next to proceed. You will not succeed if you do not.

I assume that you are intelligent. It is a fascinating statistic that in any given year, fully three-quarters of Americans will not read one single book. If you are career-minded, and you are reading this book, I am going to go ahead and assume that you do not need to be beaten over the head with a concept.

Almost anybody can write a reasonable, straightforward sentence. You do not need to be a great writer, or even a good writer, to write a great resume. Resume writing is a formula that you are going to learn. This is business writing, not literature. Know your limitations and stay within them, and your resume will come out fine.

Too much writing skill can actually be a detriment. One of the worst professional resume writers I ever hired had a Ph.D. in English. He wrote beautiful, vivid sentences that painted a picture just as clearly as Michelangelo, but these sentences made horrible resumes. The reader's attention was drawn to the writer's literary embellishments, not to the candidate's accomplishments.

The book does not create motivation—it channels it. My assumption that you are motivated to create your own success is a fairly safe one, because you have procured what is obviously a *self*-help book. On the other hand, this book is designed to make highly efficient use of your motivation.

The process of writing your own resume can be quite exhilarating. Distilling and recounting your accomplishments is intrinsically satisfying, but the impetus to begin must come from you.

If you have read to here, turn on your computer, go to the next page, and you'll have a resume in no time.

1 Why You Need a Resume

The resume is an integral part of the job-search process. Career books have been ringing the resume's death knell off and on for over twenty years, but the resume is even more popular now than ever before. I have seen good resumes for journeyman carpenters, for TV personalities, for CFOs, for management consultants, you name it. The resume can be either a stumbling block or a springboard in anyone's job search.

In the simplest terms, here's why you need a resume: **Everyone will ask you for one.**

Here's why you need it fast: **You're not the only one they will ask.**

Whether you see a cool job posting or your friend mentions they're looking for help down at her office, you need to act promptly. If writing your resume takes too long, you may miss your chance. A speedy response creates momentum especially when dealing with headhunters or tips from friends. Urgency and momentum make the hiring authority employ you instead of deciding to keep looking.

As you can probably tell, I am a big fan of resumes. Resumes have made great contributions to meritocracy and efficiency in America. We no longer live in an economy where you can go to work at Uncle Bob's gas station or Aunt Jane's conglomerate. Even if that is still done, it is no longer the model. You sell your skills to the highest bidder, presumably the one who can utilize those skills for the greatest return. And you use your resume to sell those skills.

2 What Your Resume Can Do for You

A good resume can do four things, each distinctly separate and distinctly important:

- Get the interview.
- Structure the interview.
- Remind the interviewer about you later.
- Justify the hiring decision to others.

———————

The biggest challenge your resume will ever face is direct competition, winning the interview in the shoulder-to-shoulder battle with other resumes, many of which are from candidates with better qualifications than yours. Some glamour industries, such as the hottest and most successful tech companies, receive in excess of one thousand unsolicited resumes per day. Following my guidelines, my clients have often gotten interviews and jobs at odds well in excess of one thousand to one.

Writing resumes that win interviews requires an understanding of what happens to your resume when it hits XYZ Corp. It is usually screened by resume-sorting software and then a lower-level human being whose sole reason to exist is to keep you away from any hiring managers. Management time is valuable, so these screeners act to protect it. Even if you are applying for an executive position, you must make it easy for the software and the clerk, or your application will end up in the black hole of some database.

How to write resumes is only one interview-winning key in this book. In chapter 15, "How to Get Interviews and Plan and Manage a Job Search," and chapter 16, "Cover Letters: Don't Write One until You Read Chapter 15," I will show you how to avoid getting into that screening pile in the first place.

———————

Everybody knows that resumes are useful for getting interviews, but not everybody realizes the resume's other, equally important, functions: It structures the interview process, reminds the interviewer of you after you are gone, and justifies the hiring decision to others.

Most interviewers will go right down your employment history asking questions about each job. Your resume should not tell the whole story; it should pique curiosity, begging for a clarifying question. (However, it should not be confusing or obtuse.)

Incidentally, you should take plenty of extra copies of your resume to any interview. Your interviewer will often ask for one, and some interviewers ask for several as a ploy to get all of yours away from you. Then they can test your memory. Have plenty of copies and pass this test.

———————

After the interview, the resume reminds the interviewer of what you have to offer. Even professional interviewers are strongly swayed by your written presentation. Research has shown that after you are gone, the resume can overwhelm the interviewer's memory of you in person. A candidate with a good written presentation will be remembered as articulate, well groomed, and intelligent; one with a poor written presentation will be remembered as unkempt, inarticulate, and ill prepared, *regardless of how the candidates actually performed in the interview.* Few candidates realize how important this resume function is.

The one major exception to the above occurs when an interviewer decides you are lying or grossly exaggerating. In this case, all credibility is lost and your written presentation is discounted entirely. Don't cross that line.

(If you interview people, be sure to prepare the same questions for every candidate, and score each candidate's professionalism and preparedness immediately after she leaves the room. Then later, make yourself believe those scores.)

———————

Finally, your resume can justify the hiring decision to others. The hiring cycle is getting longer and longer. More people are involved, and everyone is afraid to make a mistake. If you are the wrong hire, it can be very difficult to get rid of you. There are people higher up in the organization who will rubber stamp your hire decision without ever meeting you. The better you look on paper, the more comfortable they are. Here the wrong resume can undo every right thing about you.

Time after time candidates have come into my office and said something like, "I don't need anything special; I've already got the job." My first thought is: Then why are they asking you for a resume? Somebody is not yet fully satisfied, and that resume better live up to the rest of your presentation, or the whole thing could unravel.

As you are writing your resume, keep in mind what you want it to do for you. If you understand what your goals are, what you want your resume to accomplish *each time you use it*, you will do a better job of achieving those goals.

3 The Rules of Resume Writing

The rules of resume writing are simple:

- There are no rules that cannot be broken, with cause.
- Be careful of what you want; you may get it.
- Do *not* hold back.
- Do *not* tell a lie.

Rule #1

There are no absolutes in resume writing. In other words, every rule you have ever heard about resumes can be broken if you have a compelling reason.

Rule #2

Be careful of what you want; you may get it. This ancient Chinese proverb is as valid today as ever. Think about what you really want. More money, more power, and more responsibility are not always as much fun as you think, especially with the wrong company.

Rule #3

Do not hold back. This is one of the few times in your life when blowing your own horn is exactly what you are supposed to do. If you are timid, force yourself to think of how your spouse or best friend might describe your skills and accomplishments.

If you state your skills and accomplishments well and accurately, you will increase your chances of getting a job that will maximize your potential. This is good for you, and it is good for society. So don't hold back.

Rule #4

Do not, I repeat, *do not* tell a lie. A blatant lie on your resume is the biggest mistake you can make. Besides, it reveals a lack of creativity. The "problem" you feel compelled to lie about can be solved another way. Headhunters and companies check the basic facts on resumes, and there are consulting firms whose sole job it is to do this. If you still are not convinced, consider the following.

I had a mid-level candidate who lied to me about a college degree, which I then put in his resume. He had a great interview with the CEO. He had a great interview with the president. He thought he had the job. The president and the CEO agreed. They decided on $90,000 for a first-year compensation package. He went to the director of human resources to fill out the papers and she said, "You know, I called your college and they have no record of you." The irony here is that neither the president nor the CEO was a college graduate. No one will hire a liar.

Then, I had a candidate who lied brazenly on her application, claiming a technical skill she did not have (the ability weld aluminum, to be exact). To her credit, she learned the skill on the job in her first few weeks. Her ambition and talent allowed her to move off the shop floor and into management.

Seventeen years later, she got friendly with a coworker and bragged about her feat. You can guess the rest of the story. She got into a fight with her friend, and the friend went to top management. She was summarily fired. Company policy. No one will retain a liar.

A lie can come back to haunt you for years and years and years. Even if it gets you hired, it is not worth it.

There are no other rules. It is absolutely *not* true that your resume must be one page. Your resume is first and foremost a business document. It should be long enough to establish what you have to offer, and short enough to entice the reader to want to know more. It should not be more than two pages without a good reason (and there are many). It should have big enough print to be easily read. It should include roughly ten years of experience unless more or less is to your benefit. All the important points should be introduced on the first page if it is more than one page. It should be submitted in Adobe (.pdf) or MS Word (.doc or .docx) format, unless you're given other instructions. The print version should go on white or off-white paper unless you are in the creative end of one of the visual arts. These are all useful points, but they are far from rules.

4 Resume English Simplified

Start Each Sentence with an Action Verb

Do not be boring! Be excited about yourself! Use hard-driving language! "Handled" is a ho-hum verb, but "orchestrated" is a vivid, thought- and image-provoking verb. Although your resume should not read like a war novel, use evocative verbs whenever possible.

Effective Resume Verbs

Create	Implement	Schedule	Install	Administer	Attain
Design	Revise	Motivate	Analyze	Oversee	Evaluate
Manage	Reorganize	Coordinate	Prepare	Guide	Streamline
Supervise	Troubleshoot	Act as liaison*	Teach	Execute	Maximize
Direct	Overhaul	Select	Promote	Conduct	Facilitate
Establish	Resolve	Compile	Increase	Provide	Contribute
Plan	Initiate	Produce	Test	Generate	Consolidate
Devise	Originate	Ensure**	Start	Advise	Utilize
Organize	Train	Reconcile	Orchestrate	Develop	Negotiate

*"Liaise" as a verb is a backformation; "act as liaison" is better usage.
**More exact than "insure."

There is no magic to any of these verbs. You should use words you are comfortable with, but if you get stuck at any point in writing your resume, just browse through this list. You'll find an exciting way to describe your experiences.

Sentence structures to avoid, however, are "responsible for . . ." and "duties included . . ." Remove these passive constructions and start your sentence with a verb, and you'll have a *much* better line. "Duties included managing a staff of seven, opening and closing the store, and the nightly cash count" becomes "Managed staff of seven. Opened and closed the store. Conducted the nightly cash count." That's much better.

Be Precise

Be exact whenever you can! Use precise numbers and specific nouns. To a seasoned resume reader, "supervised staff" has a slippery feel. On the other hand, "supervised three project engineers (team leaders), seven design and mechanical engineers, and 22 technical support personnel" gives the reader a lot of confidence in the truth of your resume.

Every time you can specify a figure, you increase the verifiability of your resume. It is a point of psychology that more people will believe an exact figure than a rounded one. A resume is probably one of the only places in the known universe where $9.65 million is greater than $10 million. Exactitude makes the readers comfortable with your claims.

The old rule from secretarial school was to spell out numbers one through ten, and use Arabic numerals for 11 and over. In a resume, however, using 2, 3, 4, and so on makes for a good, businesslike read. Just be sure to use one system or the other throughout the document. I prefer "$350,000" to "$350K" but it's probably not critical, again, as long as you do it one way or the other consistently. "$350,000,000" is very impressive written out fully, but it is a bit pretentious if everyone in your field would have written "$350 million." Use your own judgment. Incidentally, on international resumes "US$350 million" means "350 million *United States* dollars," an important distinction.

Search for the Superlative

Superlatives are compelling. I cannot emphasize this enough. You are the "first," "only," "most," or "best" something, I guarantee it. Be creative. Here are some superlatives:

- Top producer companywide, out of over 100 full-time sales professionals.
- Ranked #1 in the office for customer satisfaction.
- First account executive in the nation to sign an order for our off-site storage system.
- Managed the fastest-growing enterprise group on the West Coast.
- Merchandised the most profitable line in the company.
- Had the lowest error rate in the department.

and so on . . .

Observe the following transitions, each better than the last:

- Traveled to Boston for client meeting.
- Traveled to Boston *with senior management* for client meeting.
- *Selected to* travel to Boston with senior management for client meeting.
- *Only intern* selected to travel to Boston with senior management for client meeting.

Use Insiders' Language

Baseball players do not normally use the term "batting practice." They say "BP." Similarly, the "players" in the financial world don't say "mergers and acquisitions" inside their own offices. They discuss "M&A activities." Use of insiders' language is a critical way of identifying that you are in fact an insider.

So, contrary to what other resume books say on this issue, I encourage you to use jargon and abbreviations. Use them judiciously, but do use them. The test is simple: If everyone on the inside will know what you mean, go ahead; if the jargon might seem foreign to those on the inside, leave it out. Do not forget that your own company's most common jargon may be unintelligible outside your office walls. That is the type of jargon to avoid.

So if you're trying to get out of the military and go into a defense contractor, some DoD jargon can stay in (such as "DoD"). If you're trying to get out of the military and into the non-military worlds of business, education, nonprofit, or government, it's all got to be translated into English they'll understand. So, "platoon" becomes "team," "soldiers" becomes "staff" or "employees" or "subordinates." Materiél such as MRAPs and A-10s or Warthogs becomes "equipment." It is jargon the reader will understand that is okay. For more on this, check out this web site for transitioning military: www.destinygroup.com.

Some abbreviations are pretty common in most business settings. Here are a few examples of abbreviations and jargon that I think are useable in almost any resume. They have the benefit of being efficient, and can give your resume a hard-driving feel: CEO, COO, CFO, LOC or L/C, A/P, A/R, RFP, ROI, P&L, T&E, CPA, IP, CIO, IT and most of the 5,324 other most common technology terms. If these are not familiar to you, then they are not insiders' language to you, and you should consider not using them. If you know them and use them in a normal business setting, then put them into your resume fearlessly.

Finally, if you are a design engineer appointed to the Space Suit Topographical Reconnaissance Inquiry Panel (SSTRIP), spell it out one time and then list the acronym in parentheses (as I just did). Thereafter you can just call it SSTRIP.

Write a Letter to Your Sister for a First Draft

If you write a letter to your sister about your job accomplishments, it will be a great first draft of your resume. All your sentences will make sense, the verb tenses will be correct, and you won't have to worry about the grammar police.

For example, here is the letter to your sister:

I have been part of the start-up management team for Repeat Advertising, a global advertising art recycling company. I report to the president. I serve as the chief administrative officer (CAO). I participate in all strategic business planning functions. I have contributed to the phenomenal success of this company, from a small entrepreneurial firm to a $22 million international company with 100 employees and four offices (New York, London, Shanghai, Tokyo). I directed the start-up of a subsidiary, Repeat Sound, a library of original music and sounds for rent by advertising agencies worldwide. I conducted the feasibility study for this start-up, collaborated with IT on the design of our sound vault and retrieval system, and designed the initial marketing push. I collaborated with our legal staff on global copyright and IP law.

Now, to turn your first draft into traditional resume language, just take out some of the words to create that clipped business style that is traditional for resumes.

- Take out most references to yourself, such as "I," "we," "my," and "our." You can occasionally use an "I" or a "we" to emphasize a point, but most of these can go.

- Take out some appearances of "a," "an," and "the." That makes it zippy.

- Remove these words unless doing so distorts the meaning: "am," "is," "are," "were," "be," "been," and "have," "had," "may," "might." Occasionally a transition will sound better with one of these words in place, but most of them can go.

- Look for any other words that are unnecessary. If you can throw them out without changing the meaning, do so.

Very quickly this will come naturally to you. So, here's the letter to a sister with most of these words marked out:

~~I have been~~ part of the start-up management team for Repeat Advertising, a global advertising art recycling company. ~~I~~ report to the president. ~~I~~ serve as ~~the~~ chief administrative officer (CAO). ~~I~~ participate in all strategic business planning functions. ~~I have~~ contributed to the phenomenal success of this company, from ~~a~~ small entrepreneurial firm to ~~a~~ $22 million international company with 100 employees and four offices (New York, London, Shanghai, Tokyo). ~~I~~ directed ~~the~~ start-up of a subsidiary, Repeat Sound, a library of original music and sounds for rent by advertising agencies worldwide. ~~I~~ conducted the feasibility study for this start-up, collaborated with IT on the design of our sound vault and retrieval system, and designed ~~the~~ initial marketing push. ~~I~~ collaborated with ~~our~~ legal ~~staff~~ on global copyright and IP law.

Voilà, here's how it reads on the resume:

Part of the start-up management team for Repeat Advertising, a global advertising art recycling company. Report to the president. Serve as chief administrative officer (CAO). Participate in all strategic business planning functions. Contributed to the phenomenal success of this company, from small entrepreneurial firm to $22 million international company with 100 employees and four offices (New York, London, Shanghai, Tokyo). Directed start-up of a subsidiary, Repeat Sound, a library of original music and sounds for rent by advertising agencies worldwide. Conducted the feasibility study for this start-up, collaborated with IT on the design of our sound vault and retrieval system, and designed initial marketing push. Collaborated with legal on global copyright and IP law.

Note that current and ongoing duties are in the present tense, and past projects and accomplishments are in the past tense.

Here's another first draft:

I am the assistant manager in charge of store operations for the Round Tire Co. I am in charge of customer service and staff supervision on a day-to-day basis. Some of my accomplishments include reducing headcount by three with a concurrent increase in sales, establishing a new safety compliance program that reduced our insurance costs, and resolving a Department of Environmental Quality (DEQ) complaint about our tire storage procedures. Also initiated a free rotation promotion which brought in increased revenues.

Here's the final draft, with extra words removed, more precise numbers and information, a superlative added in, and sentences restructured to begin with action verbs:

Round Tire Co.
Assistant Manager
Direct all aspects of store operations on a day-to-day basis. Oversee customer service. Schedule and supervise a staff of 7 to 15 per shift.
Accomplishments:

- Reduced headcount by 3 with a concurrent increase in sales.

- Established new safety compliance program resulting in reduced insurance costs.

- Resolved a Department of Environmental Quality (DEQ) complaint about our tire storage procedures.

- Created a "free rotation" promotion, resulting in $12,000 increase in sales per month in brake and suspension repairs. This was the store's most successful promotion over the last year.

To sum up: Tenses should be accurate, and you are the (unstated) subject of most sentences. **Write the first draft of your resume as though it were a letter to your sister.** Avoid complex sentence constructions. If you follow these guidelines, your English will be fine.

5 Writing Your Resume: Style Overview

The Two Major Styles of Resume: Chronological & Functional

Although there are hundreds of variations in resume styles, there are two major and fairly incompatible families of resume: the chronological and the functional. In short, a chronological resume lists each job with a complete listing, that is, employer, title, dates, duties, and accomplishments. The listings are assembled in reverse chronological order, with the most recent job listed first. The functional style of resume lumps skills or accomplishments together under headings such as "Management" or "Fundraising," then lists all the positions and employers at the bottom, with or without dates.

The first person to develop and use a functional resume was undoubtedly a resume genius. It is absolutely the most effective style for managing an unorthodox career, a complex work history, and other resume "problems." However, anybody with a logical or coherent work history should use some version of the chronological style. There are two very good reasons for this: functional resumes are difficult to write, and many employers hate them.

Why would an employer hate a resume style? Because it is too good at hiding candidates' weaknesses. Consequently, candidates with problems gravitate to this style. Any experienced interviewer has wasted time interviewing unqualified applicants with intentionally deceptive functional resumes.

For example, under the "MANAGEMENT" heading a functional resume may say:

Supervised staff of 12. Gave daily assignments and monitored quality of work performance. Planned and executed comprehensive marketing campaigns.

Then, under "EMPLOYMENT" it may list:

V.P., Marketing, XYZ Software Development Corp.

But when it comes time to interview the candidate for head of a corporate marketing department, the interviewer discovers that the "staff of 12" were all pizza delivery drivers, and the candidate was all of 19 years old at the time; and XYZ Software Corp. was a startup pipe dream, staff of two (i.e., this candidate and, of course, the co-founder of XYZ). This is what can happen when accomplishments are divorced from positions and employers.

From your own point of view as a resume writer, functional resumes are difficult to get "just right." It takes a wordsmith to excel in this style. I personally have the highest regard for the functional resume, and we do write them occasionally in my office, but you are better off if you can sell yourself successfully with a chronological resume.

The bulk of my background is with a fast-track management clientele, and they usually do have coherent backgrounds. This book concentrates on variations of the chronological style that are common, conservative, and successful for my clients.

There is such a thing as a resume in the third person. Sentences will read something like this: "William Smith possesses the highest standards of professional integrity . . ." Headhunters popularized this style in writing about their candidates, but I feel it is stilted, at best. It is, however, a good way to write a consultant's resume. We'll have more on this in chapter 14, "Special Styles, More Solutions."

Control Your Reader's Eye

Your resume is a design project as well as a writing project. The words have to look good together, regardless of what they say. As you write your resume, you must also design it. It should look good at arm's length, and it should control your reader's eye. To accomplish this, use emphasis judiciously. Emphasizers that can help you control the reader's eye are bold type, italics, underlining, font size, and capitalization. Note: do not mix too many different emphasizers on a page, as the result can be dizzying. Here is a table of descending emphasis:

BOLD ALL CAPS
REGULAR ALL CAPS
Upper- and Lowercase Bold
Title-Style Capitalization of Major Words with Upper- and Lowercase Letters
Sentence-style capitalization for first words, followed by lowercase letters
Italics, only for book titles, foreign words, and special emphasis

Mixing fonts is to be avoided. It always seems like a good idea at the time, but ends up looking weird.

When I want to control the eye of the reader, I will use emphasis out of the expected order. Note the following:

The University of Arkansas, Fayetteville, Arkansas
B.S., Chemistry, 2010

The reader's eye skips the school and concentrates on the degree and major.
Compare with this:

STANFORD UNIVERSITY, Stanford, California
B.A., Art History, 2010

See how different these two listings are? Although in many ways identical, what is emphasized controls what the reader reads, and its impact on her. Here are two more samples, just for fun:

New York University, New York, New York
B.S. candidate, **Business Administration,** ongoing

International Business, Wharton School of Business, 2010
University of Pennsylvania, Philadelphia

If the emphasis is effective enough, readers will read something not actually written on the page. This is just effective resume design.

One warning, however: You must be consistent in your design choices. If you bold one university, you must bold them all in the same way. If you put one job title in italics, you must put them all in italics. If you list one state using a postal code, as in NY, CT, or CA, then you must do so in all parallel constructions. If you list one date year to year, as in 2009–2011, you must list them all year to year, and not start specifying months somewhere else as (10/2006–5/2008). If you list numbers under 10 as numerals, 4, 5, 6, and so on, then you can't revert to spelling out one, two, three someplace else in the resume. **Inconsistency is considered a sign of a lack of intelligence.** You can't afford for someone to think you're not too bright because you mix up design choices! Your design consistency makes a statement about you as a potential employee, about your detail skills, about your marketing sense, and about your ability to do a simple assignment.

Also, be aware of the balance of the material on your page, and how it looks at arm's length. This is determined by word groupings, or listings, and the space between them. The mind loves a list of three, likes a list of two, and is not too happy with a list of more than four. You can be sure that no reader is going to be eager to read a resume without sufficient white space. And if your readers are over 40, you'd better not choose any fonts under 12 pt. size.

This is a pretty listing:

- Nec mora, cum omnibus illis cibariis uasculis raptim remotis.

- Laciniis cunctis suis renundata crinibusque dissolutis ad.

- Hilarem lasciuiam in speciem Veneris, quae marinos.

- Fluctus subit, pulchre reformata, paulisper.

This is a pretty listing:

- Etiam glabellum feminal rosea palmula potius obumbrans de industria quam tegens uerecundia: proeliare, inquit, et fortiter.

- Proeliare, nec enim tibi cedam nec terga uortam; comminus in aspectum si uir es, derige et grassare nauiter et occide moriturus.

But very few readers will want to wade through a block of text more than five lines deep:

- Hodierna pugna non habet missionem. Haec simul dicens inscenso grabattulo super me sessim residens ac credbra subsiliens lubricisque gestibus mobilem spinam quatiens pendulae Veneris fructu me satiauit, usque dum lassis animis et marcidis artibus defatigati simul ambo corruimus inter mutuos amplexus animas hanhelantes. His et huius modi conluctationibus ad confinia lucis usque peruigiles egimus poculis interdum lassitudinem refouentes et libidinem incitantes et uoluptatem integrantes. Ad cuius noctis exemplar similes adstruximus alias plusculas, ad infinitum.

Executive resumes can have longer blocks of type, but unless you're well north of $100,000, I'd avoid it. At the other end of the spectrum, as a general rule avoid the style of using a bullet for *every single sentence* in the resume. I call this the Teflon™ resume: It reads fast but nothing sticks in the mind. This style is popular on some college campuses, but unless you're a college student, I'd skip it. Mixing up a little paragraph formatting with some bulleted lists is a little more sophisticated. You'll see that most of the examples in this book follow that format. Finally, I am not a fan of the style of putting your headings in the center of the page. We read from left to right, so put your headings on the left margin. Don't make your reader bounce back and forth from margin to center, as if they were watching a tennis match. Your name and address can be centered, but after that start headings on the left margin.

So, while you are writing your resume, design it as you go along. It is much more difficult to fix the design than it is to do it right the first time.

Control your reader's eye. Balance the look of your resume on the page.

6 Writing Your Resume: The One Thing You MUST Do First

Point of View: Who Is This Thing for, Anyway?

Every employer has a sentence stenciled on the inside of her eyelids: "What can this candidate do for me?" Every time she blinks her eyes, she sees this sentence. It is a question you had better answer.

This is "point of view." *Her* point of view, and the one you are going to think about as you write and design your resume. A resume is not a summary of your life, a chance to list accomplishments important to you, or a representation of your social and political values. It is an attempt to answer that question on the inside of the employer's eyelids: "What can this candidate do for me?"

As you write, you are going to adopt your next employer's point of view. You are going to anticipate her concerns, guess what would excite her, and envision her motivations. You are going to get inside her head.

Children cannot do this, cannot get outside of their own egos, but you can. You are an adult. You can foresee this employer reading your resume. You can feel the paper, you can see her read, and you can feel her think. *You can adopt her point of view.*

I am going to ask you to adopt a point of view outside of yourself several times. Take it very seriously. It is the key to good writing of any kind, and it is the key to **great** resumes.

The One Thing You MUST Do First

The one thing you must do first is envision the ideal candidate. Forget about yourself entirely. Sit down, take out a fresh sheet of paper, and write down what you envision about the ideal candidate for the job you want. This is one of the most important techniques you will learn in this book. If you will do this now, the rest of your project will flow like water down the mountain.

What **features, attributes, traits, skills,** and **strengths** do you envision in this ideal candidate? Close your eyes and "see" this ideal candidate at work. See her plan and execute. See her accomplish. See her win. See her make her company happy. As you do this, write down what you see immediately as it occurs to you.

As an exercise, let us do this for two positions: a sales representative and an accounting manager. Both positions are open at Acme Web Design, a small e-commerce consulting firm with 29 employees and just under $7 million in revenues.

Sales Representative. The first thing I see is a smile, and it is a real smile, not a fake one. So, let's write, "friendly and outgoing personality." A related skill that comes to mind would be "never forgets a name or a face." Next, I see this sales rep working alone, so I might jot down, "able to be effective working alone, without direct supervision." Right away, I think of "able to plan and execute a sales campaign independently," "able to develop a winning sales presentation from scratch." And I think of related administrative tasks that fall on those of us who work alone, so I write, "able to organize, track, and control a heavy work flow," and "strong follow-through on details."

Then, I see this sales rep trying to crack a new account, and I think how hard it is to penetrate the screen around top executives, so I might write, "able to access the top management of targeted companies." I start to think of how sophisticated the sale is to this level of client, and I see a sales rep who is smart and analytical, who "can develop sophisticated cost-benefit analyses showing the bottom-line advantages of Acme Web Design." Suddenly I remember that this person has to work with the tech people at the client company and at our firm, so I write "able to serve as a liaison between client company technology officers and e-commerce architects."

Suddenly it occurs to me that I do not want to risk my most important new accounts on a newcomer to sales, so I want somebody with a "proven track record of success" or "demonstrated talent at opening new accounts and launching new lines of business." And I want repeat sales, too, so I write, "history of very high rates for repeat and referral business."

I am having a lot of fun with this hypothetical sales rep—we are sitting at a conference table adding up fat profits for the last quarter—when I suddenly start to think of things that could go wrong. Maybe this super-talented sales rep starts to look like an ego problem to me, so I jot down, "outstanding references from all former employers" and "ability to fit into an organization and be productive immediately," which are different ways of saying that this rep is a "team player."

Finally, in addition to gross sales, I want organizational contributions from this sales rep. I want someone who "can train new account executives" and "can build new marketing channels" for Acme. That would be ideal.

Accounting Manager. Again, close your eyes and see this ideal accounting manager. My own accounting manager is so trustworthy I let her run my business, so the first things I will write are "trustworthy" and "able to meet management objectives without direct supervision." Then I think in rapid succession, "knows popular accounting and spreadsheet software," "able to learn and implement new software from documentation alone," "able to design new statements, reports and operating procedures as needed," and "able to plan and control work flow in a deadline environment."

Just to be sure we don't miss some technical skill, let's make a laundry list of talent for our ideal candidate: "general ledger, accounts payable, accounts receivable, payroll, multistate payroll, commission accounting, cost accounting, fixed-asset accounting, cash report, quarterly and year-end report, annual profit-and-loss report, balance sheet, you name it."

Since Acme is a small firm, this accounting manager is also most likely the de facto chief financial officer. So the ideal accounting manager would be "able to serve as the company representative to banks, CPAs, the IRS, and vendors." Acme is probably run by a technician/founder, someone who is a good design engineer and strategic decision maker, but who doesn't want to get bogged down in the details of business administration. So Acme would benefit from an accounting manager who could "support strategic decision-making through timely access to financial and other data."

Finally, since we are dealing with the ideal candidate, I will even write, "never makes a mistake."

Take the time now to envision the ideal candidate for your next position. Again, *this has nothing to do with you.* Have an open mind, see the candidate in action, think the ideal candidate's thoughts, take the employer's point of view, and make a list of **features, attributes, traits, skills,** and **strengths.**

Do not read further until you have done this. When you are satisfied that you have done your best, only then should you set aside your notes and turn to the next chapter.

Words to Include

If you have a position description or a posted opening, look for the words that describe the skills and experiences the employer is seeking. If they were going to plug the announcement into a search engine, *which terms would they use?* No one is going to search for "good manager" or "someone able to execute effectively," so you can skip all the usual drivel that would apply equally to a security guard or an executive.

Look for words that are not routine. Look for the *unique* words, such as "nosocomial infection" (an infection that a patient incurs while in the hospital) or "tribology" (an engineering term for the study of friction) or "cohousing" (a type of cooperative housing development), or specific software releases, such as "Wombat 2.9," or language skills, "bilingual or fluent in Spanish a plus." Make a list of these terms. Add any other search terms that you can imagine they might use, such as "B.A.," or "M.B.A.," or "CPA" or whatever. You have to imagine, or guess, what search terms they might use. It is not unusual for employers to search for certain schools or former employers by name.

You have to find ways to get these words into your resume.

You also have to imagine all the forms or combinations of the search terms the employer might use. For example, they may search for "accounts receivable" or they may search for "A/R," so find a way to put both into your resume: "managed accounts receivable (A/R)." Or maybe you think they'll search for "M.B.A.," and you have a "Master of Human Resources and Organization Development." On your resume you'd want to find a formula to list it the way they'll search for it:

University of San Francisco, San Francisco, California

Master of Human Resources and Organization Development

(equivalent to M.B.A. Human Resources)

A truly creative person can find ways to say almost anything, truthfully, while getting the right search terms into the resume:

LANGUAGES:

Spanish (basic proficiency now, but I would love to become fluent in Spanish in the future)

You see how a computer will read this, right? I don't have to spell this out for you, right? You may not be able to get all the terms into your resume, but pack in as many as you can.

7 Writing Your Resume: Getting Started with the Heading

The Heading

You may think this is a ridiculously obvious part of the resume, but I do have a few significant points about it that seem to interest people when I lecture.

You need to start with your name, address, phone, and email. If your name is going to be difficult for the reader, consider adopting a nickname, as in this example:

Wei-Wen "Wendy" Lee

If your name is William Zebulon Harrison Styles, and everyone in the world knows you as Buddy Styles, you use a similar presentation:

William Z. H. "Buddy" Styles

However, if you live in the Northeast Corridor, Philadelphia-New York-Providence-Boston, nicknames are generally not listed on resumes or, indeed, on any written document. The protocol here is to wait until you are formally introduced to someone before asking them to call you by your nickname, although this is changing as regional differences are muted by worker migration.

At least let the reader know your gender, if nothing else. If your name doesn't reveal your gender, put a small "Mr." or "Ms." *after* your name, in parentheses, and in smaller type:

Zbignew Bresinski (Mr.)

That old technique of using just your initials, to reduce gender bias one way or the other, will backfire. Not knowing your gender just makes employers uncomfortable. Any employer will be reluctant to contact you if they don't know your gender.

Should you ever use a fake name? If you are going to post your resume on the Internet, some people do use a fake name and anonymous contact information (post office box for an address, untraceable email and cell phone). There are plenty of good reasons to do this, and employers are now familiar with this phenomenon. You are not weird for wanting to conceal your identity on the Internet. So consider this option, especially if you're concerned about stalkers or your own employer finding your posting. You can change the name of your employer too, to something generic. So "google" becomes "a search engine technology provider" and "Wal-Mart" becomes "a major discount retailer."

Employers will usually make first contact via email. Since your employer owns your company email address *and all the mail you send and receive on it,* it is usually not a great idea to use your work email for a job search. Use a private email address. So what does your private email say about you? Hotfoxy69@hotmail.com and devilboy666@gmail.com are definitely out. I know a recruiter who didn't hire a woman with butterfly24@server.com as an email address. "I liked her resume," he said, "but we're just not a 'butterfly' kind of place." Pick something nice, neutral, and businesslike.

You have to put your cell phone number on your resume, but consider listing *all* your phone numbers: home, office, and cell. When a recruiter uses the phone to make contact, they're in a hurry. Usually they will call several other people as well. They will not be calling you again if you're too hard to reach, or your roommate or your teenagers forget to write down your messages. It goes without saying that all your outgoing messages need to be short and professional during your job search.

It's a judgment call whether to put your office phone number on your resume. The advantage is that other companies can reach you at their convenience during the business day. If you don't list it, be sure to answer your cell phone during the day for the duration of your job search. One risk to listing an office number is that your current employer will discover you are looking for another position. Also, if you are leaving, or at risk of leaving, your office phone may be obsolete long before your resume is.

If your employer finds out you are looking, do not be ashamed of it. It is your right in the modern world. The covenant between employer and employee has been fundamentally rewritten in recent years. Everyone works by mutual agreement now. You may even wish to sit down with your boss and engineer your own departure. On the other hand, if you do not think your company is so progressive, do not tell even your closest confidant about your considered departure. No news travels faster, not even that of an office affair.

If you are looking nationally or internationally, consider writing "24 hours" or "24/7" next to your cell number, or invite them to text you by listing "voice or text" after your cell number. Remember, the easier it is to contact you, the more likely it is you will be contacted. For the duration of your job search, think twice before answering if you're with indiscreet friends or hanging out in a loud club.

Your mailing address is not a trivial matter, either. You need to realize they can look up your house values and even overhead and curbside pictures using google Earth and real estate web sites. If you are at all concerned about issues like these, use a post office box. By the way, if you are looking for work in a distant city, use a local address! Either borrow an address from a friend, or rent a post office or mail service box for the duration of your search. Don't worry if your resume shows a Chicago address and an employer based in Phoenix. You can explain your situation when they contact you, and believe me, you want them to contact you! Your local address shows you are serious about the community, and the employer will give you the same consideration as the other fine candidates available locally. At the middle-management level and under, this technique has proved to be the clincher for my clients again and again.

Here is how you borrow an address from your friend, John Smith:

Your Name
c/o Smith
His Street Address
His City, State, Zip

With the explosion of cell phones and area codes, it doesn't matter what phone number you use with any address. I have seen as many as three different addresses on the same resume. You can have an "East Coast address," a "West Coast address," a "permanent address," a "local address," a "school address," or an address "until June 21" and "after June 21."

By the way, use a hyphen between a numbered street and a house number: 2201-16th Street.

Finally, now that you have spent so much attention on getting your heading just the way you want it, draw a line from margin to margin underneath it. That will **control the reader's eye,** and she will not even read it. A name and address by itself never got anyone a job, and you want your precious few seconds of screening to focus on what you have to offer.

Instead of reading this book, use it now. Turn on your computer and design your heading!

Samples:

Jennifer Wilson Stone
265 Stateline View Lane
South Lake Tahoe, California 96150
Cell: (916) 555-2049 (24/7, voice/txt)
jstone@lake.com

(The reader's eye is drawn here. The resume starts here.)

Khalh N. Khorghiann (Mr.)

knk@khorghiann.com

U.S.A./permanent address:	U.K. address:	Swiss family address:
800 Pacific Heights Avenue	"The Cedar"	"Chalet Lisabeth"
Penthouse	16 Copse Hill	Champ de Moulin
Laguna Beach, California	London SW20 ONL	1296 Charmey
92651	England, U.K.	Switzerland
U.S.A.	44.82.568.6385 or	41.29.75820
(714) 555-1381	44.81.568.5816	

(The reader's eye is drawn here. The resume starts here.)

M. N. "Missy" Menendez

mm89@smu.edu

school address (until 6/2011)	local address
7845 Claiborne Way	c/o Johnson
Dallas, Texas 75246	2731 Evergreen Court
Cell: (214) 555-8545	Shoreline, Washington 98155

(The reader's eye is drawn here. The resume starts here.)

8 Writing Your Resume: Win or Lose in the First Ten Lines

Sizzle *and* Steak, Form *and* Content

The hottest resume style in use today is the profile style. It is what fast-track heavy hitters have been using for years to blow the competition out of the water. When a profile resume is done right, it is a beautiful, flawless device, the perfect marriage of form and content. Most important, it is so effective it is scary.

Why does it work so well? Because it answers that all-important question—What can this candidate do for me?—in the first ten lines. Then it goes on to let the reader know that the candidate is genuine, not a faker, in the rest of the document.

The perfect career resume has these three distinct parts: the heading, which you just wrote; the profile of what the candidate has to offer; and the chronological career history, both work and education, which is the proof that the profile is true. The profile works only because the proof is right below it. The profile and the chronological sections are a one-two knockout punch. In advertising parlance, you have the sizzle and the steak all in one place.

When you answer the all-important question in the first ten lines, you are doing everybody a very big favor:

- Your resume will be sorted into the "yes" pile *without even being read.*

- Your resume will be routed to the hiring authority *without even being read.*

- Whenever it is read, it will be reviewed with focused interest *right from the top.*

- Obviously, this saves everybody a lot of time; you are capitalizing on the fact that screeners take only seconds to screen resumes. You have actually made an asset out of the biggest problem most other resumes face.

The Profile of a Winner

It is common knowledge that your resume is an advertisement for you. In advertising, the profile is what is known as the "hook," the lines at the top of an advertisement that get you to read the copy underneath. There are car ads in national magazines with as many as five hundred words in them, about the same number as in a two-page executive resume. All these ads have a hook at the top, for example, "WOULD YOU DO THIS TO YOUR KIDS?" Otherwise, no one would ever read those five hundred words. It is the same with your resume.

The names for a profile section may vary, but your heading could be any of the following:

PROFILE

INTERESTS

EXPERTISE

STRENGTHS

AREAS OF SKILL & KNOWLEDGE

So how do you write this magic bullet? Simple. First, make a subheading that describes your *functional area of expertise,* such as "Secretary/Administrative Assistant/Executive Assistant" or "Sales/ Account Management." You could use a title, "Accounting Manager," but a *functional area of expertise* gives you more latitude, as in "Accounting Management." Remember, one company's "Controller" is another's "Accounting Manager" is another's "Head of Accounting." By using a broadly worded target you will be in the running no matter what the company calls the position.

If you are interested in more than one type of job, you must choose which to focus on in this resume (you can focus on the others in later versions). You must target your resume from the top line down. Every single word is selected according to the following formula:

Put your information in order of interest to your targeted reader.

For every distinctly different type of job you seek, you will need to have a distinctly different resume.

So, you've finished your heading and drawn a line from margin to margin. You've decided what your immediate target is. You are now trying to get the attention of a busy resume screener in a matter of a second or two. Write your profile heading and your functional subheading now. Do not worry about doing this perfectly; you can always change it later.

Here're three more samples to get you started:

PROFILE

    Real Estate Sales—Residential, Commercial, Industrial

INTERESTS

    Web Page Design/e-Commerce/Search Optimization Strategies

EXPERTISE

    ZEON Reliability Engineering

———————

Then, once you have selected a heading and functional area of expertise, answer the million-dollar question in the employer's mind: "What can this candidate do for me?" Go back to your notes on the ideal candidate, circle the skills and attributes that you actually have, and make them into a little paragraph or sequence of bulleted statements. Remember, you are the subject of each sentence: "I am able to . . .," "I have nine years of experience at . . .," "I have a solid grasp of . . ."

Do not claim skills that you do not possess. If you cannot find the pen you were just using, please do not claim you are "well organized and systematic." If you have to check your bank balance online before writing a check, please do not claim to be "good with figures." If you are terrified to deal with strangers, *please* do not claim you have a "strong sales aptitude" or a "friendly, outgoing personality."

Make precise skills claims. Every grouch thinks he has a sense of humor, and every manager in business thinks he has "excellent written and oral communication skills." If you want to tell me about your communication skills, tell me that you have the "ability to design and deliver DOT-compliant driver safety training programs" or that you are "bilingual, French-English, including translating technical and legal documents into/out of either language." Prove you have technical, insiders' knowledge of the targeted industry. Avoid making a list of vague general business skills that would apply to everyone or anyone.

Remember, you are answering the question "What can this candidate do for me?" directly. You are listing **features, attributes, traits, skills,** and **strengths.** You may choose to include accomplishments or experiences, but remember that experience alone is not what the employer wants to buy; she wants to buy the *skills* that should come with that experience. And remember, thirty-five years of experience is also "more than fifteen years of experience." Don't let anyone know you are ninety-five years old. And keep it short, less than ten lines.

Use every opportunity to slant your resume to your future. You can write a profile that begins "Interest: Real Estate Sales" even if all your sales experience is in career dresses—or vice versa. Be sure to differentiate *ability* from *experience*. "I have the ability to run a marathon" is a totally different statement from "I have experience running a marathon." (This is a full-fledged resume trick; do not use it unless you really can run a marathon, if you get my point.)

Technical resumes work exactly like nontechnical resumes. They feature the candidate's skills and abilities right at the top. The trend is away from laundry lists of skills in dozens of different systems, applications, and platforms, and toward a claim of greater expertise in a few areas. If you still want to include a massive laundry list, you can put it toward the bottom of your resume under a heading "TECHNICAL SKILLSET."

"Profile" Replaces the "Objective"

Note that this heading and skills *profile* entirely replaces the old notion of an *objective*. You are offering your expertise, not acting as a supplicant for a position. My favorite resume sin is an objective like the following: "Seeking a challenging and rewarding position with a progressive company with opportunity for professional growth and advancement." Who cares!? What does this mean, anyway? Not only is it vacuous, it is permeated with the wrong point of view. "Challenging and rewarding" for whom? "Progressive" according to whom? "Professional advancement" for whom?

This does nothing to answer the employer's primary concern: "What can this candidate do for me?" Only use the "Objective" heading when you really have little or no experience or skills to offer for the targeted position. In that case, objective may be your best choice.

One last thought: Do not be tempted to use the term *entry level* in your heading, or anywhere else on your resume. It also is the wrong point of view. The job may be entry level to you, but to the hiring manager it is just another position that needs to be filled. Remember, at all levels you have skills to sell that the hiring manager wants to buy. Sell your skills. Do not beg for a job.

———————

Write the rest of your profile now, drawing from your notes on the ideal candidate. To help you get started, I have pulled a few profiles as samples. Do not read ahead in the book. Finish your first draft of your profile now. Your goal is to get every major point into your profile that you want to convey to your potential employer. Don't worry about doing this perfectly the first time! This is just a first draft. Try to get all your ideas out but don't obsess over the wording. You can always come back to your profile after you've written the rest of your resume. **Write a short profile section now,** modeled on one of the following examples.

Samples:

SKILLS

Office and Administrative Management

Ability to prioritize, delegate, and control administrative work flow to manage office or entire business. Can hire, train, and supervise support staff; design and implement policies and procedures; manage in-house accounting through quarterly reporting; provide customer service and public relations; and serve as liaison to banks, CPAs, and vendors. Proven ability to provide support to strategic decision-making through timely access to financial and other data.

———————

PROFILE

Registered Dental Hygienist

Stable and reliable, three years with current doctor, five years with prior doctor. Professional orientation is toward preventive treatment, periodontal maintenance, and patient education. Friendly, good with patients. Also experienced in office administration duties. Excellent recommendations from all doctors.

———————

EXPERTISE

Retail and Commercial Real Estate—Acquisition, Planning, Development

Strengths include cash-flow projections, valuation forecasting, highest and best use analysis, ongoing financial and economic analysis of real estate development projects, as well as presentations, negotiations, management, and oversight. Experience with both retail and commercial projects in the $10 million to $150 million range.

PROFESSION

Sales of Floor Coverings (wholesale and to-the-trade)

- 16 years in soft goods/4 years in hard goods
- 20 years of representation to architects and designers
- Background includes high-tech/commercial/industrial applications
- Proven performer with sales records on behalf of every employer

---

PROFILE

Clinical Psychologist, State of Louisiana, with expertise in the following areas:

- Business, Careers, EAP, Organizational Behavior, HPT, Coaching Teams & Groups
- Testing & Diagnostics, Executive Evaluations (pre-employment/pre-promotion)
- Workplace Violence Prevention, Crisis Intervention, Media Relations
- Sexual Harassment Prevention & Investigations
- Alcohol & Substance Abuse Issues
- Executive Coaching
- ADD/ADHD
- Effective combination of business experience, clinical knowledge, and therapeutic skill. Self-directed; comfortable with significant responsibility; able to develop programs and procedures to meet objectives; able to serve as articulate representative of employing organization.

STRENGTHS

Editing, Writing, Proofreading, Research, Pamphlet/Flier Design, Web Page Design

- Technical command of the English language: grammar, syntax, semantics, spelling, punctuation. Detailed knowledge of *The Chicago Manual of Style* and *Associated Press Stylebook.*
- Experience in copywriting, copyediting, proofreading, and production, including both print and online content.
- Studio artist with illustration and design experience. Some art direction experience, soliciting artwork and managing artists.

9 Writing Your Resume: Jobs and Dates

Education or Experience First?

If the profile is the most important part of your resume, what goes immediately beneath it is the second most important. You have two choices: education or experience. Education goes first if you have a brand-name education and you want to feature it; you are a medical doctor, a scientist, or a college professor; you have a new degree; or your education is your best qualification. Otherwise, experience comes before education. If you choose to list your education first, skip to the next chapter, write it first, then come back to list your experience. Either way, you can always switch it later.

Remember this simple rule: **Put your information in order of interest to your targeted reader.**

Experience

Before you even start, you must know that this section can include part-time experience, paid or unpaid internships, volunteer experiences, temporary positions, and sometimes even experience gained in a classroom setting. Those entering or reentering the job market and those seeking to engineer a career transition will find this point of tremendous benefit. Most of us have job experience, but if it will bolster your candidacy, consider including some of these other experiences as well as, or even instead of, your primary job experience.

The following are all possible headings for this section. Choose one and write it onto your resume *now*. Remember, this is just a first draft.

EXPERIENCE

EMPLOYMENT

HISTORY

PROFESSIONAL HISTORY

HIGHLIGHTS

Your job subheadings underneath should include name of company, title, city, and date. Here's just one example:

ACME ROCKET SUPPLIES	Chicago, IL
Assistant Export Manager	2009–2011

As mentioned on p. 20, if you are concerned your current employer will find your resume somehow, you can disguise both your name and the name of your employer. Use a descriptive title for your employer, as in these examples: "A Major Reinsurance Brokerage," "A National Auto Parts Distributor," "An Independent CPA Firm," or "A Management Consulting Group."

Dates are generally listed year to year, although students may list employment as "Summer 2010" or "Fall 2009." Listing the months you worked is just too much information that does nothing to sell you. De-emphasize the dates by putting them toward the right margin. If seniority is your greatest asset, you are looking for work in the wrong millennium. That style of putting the dates down the left margin was popular two generations ago!

Never fudge your dates of employment, as it is extremely easy for an employer to verify your dates of employment. If you want to learn how to overcome employment gaps and other special problems, see the next chapter, "Writing Your Resume: What to Do about Common Problems," and chapter 14, "Special Styles, More Solutions."

Do not include your employer's street address, names of supervisors, contact telephone numbers, reasons for leaving, salary, or other extraneous data.

Control your reader's eye! Be stingy with your use of bold as an emphasizer. Human resume screeners will read anything written in bold, so don't bold dates, cities, or other boring stuff. You do not want your reader to get bored before she even finds out what a great job you did.

Leave cities out if they show you've moved all over the country recently or that most of your experience is in other countries, or if they present any other problem. Listing cities is optional, except for the usual warning that you will want to list either *all* of them or *none,* to be consistent.

Always list your title accurately, as this is also extremely easy for a prospective employer to verify. If your real title is boring, misleading, or nondescriptive, you may use a functional title, but even then it is a good idea to list your official title in parentheses. Here is an example:

Laboratory Manager (Senior Technician IV)

Remember, don't bold the boring part.

You will list jobs in reverse chronological order, which means starting with your current or most recent position, and going backward from there. You can also divide your experience into sections, if that will help you organize the information in order of interest to your targeted reader. So if you are applying for a teaching or training job, you could put all those positions together under a heading such as "TEACHING & TRAINING ASSIGNMENTS," and put the rest of your background further down under "ADDITIONAL EXPERIENCE," or you can separate your "SALES EXPERIENCE" from your "GENERAL MANAGEMENT EXPERIENCE," and so on. Some of the resume samples later in the book are organized this way.

To create a compelling resume, your experience listing must feature **scope of authority** and **accomplishments** more than routine duties or responsibilities. Do not use a position description as a source document to write a resume. Listing routine duties and responsibilities might win a support position, but to compete for a management assignment you had better describe some solid, specific accomplishments.

Scope of authority is composed of your title and the title of the person to whom you report directly; the size of the company, product line, or division in which you work, measured in dollars if possible; the industry you are in; the technologies you use to accomplish your work; and the number of people you supervise and their titles and functions.

Prospective employers need a picture of where you worked in their minds as they read about your background. If it is not obvious, you may need to typify or otherwise depict the company you worked for, as part of your scope statement, for example: "Loran Systems is a $21 million manufacturer of automotive aftermarket products with production plants in Ohio, Indiana, Mexico, and Ireland."

Accomplishments are everything you did right. Throw away your position description and your flowcharts and let the reader know what you did *above and beyond* the minimum requirements. Your accomplishments section can include problems you solved, special projects, special assignments, training, travel, commendations, awards, and honors—anything that makes you special compared to all the other people ever to hold your title.

Ideally, you want to quantify contributions to the bottom line, even if your immediate task seemed far from financial. Perhaps you are a programmer who created an asset-tracking application that allowed a 5 percent reduction in production materials owned by the company. So, if the company owned $100 million dollars in materials, you can truthfully report that you "saved the company $5,000,000" with your application.

Even if you are "chief floor sweeper," you should be able to report *and quantify* your contributions. Think like a manager. What do they care about? Here's an example: "Requisitioned 12-inch broom to replace 10-inch broom, creating a 20 percent increase in sweeping efficiency." Get it?

The classic formula for accomplishment is PSR, Problem → Solution → Result, hopefully with a dollar value on the result. In practice, however, you can list resume accomplishments in thousands of different forms. Think, be creative, and be brief.

Explore different ways to represent the same basic fact. You can compare your performance to currently employed colleagues, to people in other departments, to prior employees, to people at other companies, and so on, virtually ad infinitum.

Let us suppose you are writing this resume because you just got fired. You were fired for lack of sales, because you only sold $1,000 worth of sackbuts (a type of trombone). But wait, the account executive before you was fired, too, after having sold only $500 worth. Let's face it—sackbuts are not very popular. Looks to me like you can say *in all honesty:* "Achieved 100 percent increase in sales for the territory, over prior sales rep." Never tell a lie, but it is your job to tell the best side of the truth.

Be sure to include **intangible accomplishments.** Tangible accomplishments are figure based, and can be verified rather easily, as in "increased sales by 38 percent in first 6 months on the job." An intangible accomplishment is not figure based and may be a little harder to verify. Here are some examples of intangible accomplishments:

- Improved staff morale and reduced turnover.

- Improved image of the product line and the company.

- Saved several "shaky" accounts and improved account loyalty.

- Contributed improvements to record-keeping systems and office operations.

Putting Scope and Accomplishments Together into Job Listings

Now you have all the components of a job listing: the company, your title, the scope of your job, and your accomplishments. Each job listing on your resume should stack these components according to this formula:

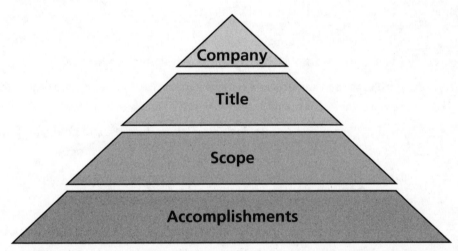

As you construct the job listings for the draft of your resume, you must decide what to include. This process has a formula: **Throw out the obvious,** then rank the rest in order of appeal to your reader.

Remember your reader? Close your eyes and see that reader, someone able to give you the job you want. See that sentence on the inside of her eyelids, "What can this candidate do for me?" See her reading your list of points. See what she will view as obvious and skip it. See what she will be most impressed by or interested in and feature it.

Obviously, the order in which you put things is up to you. You are not bound by the FDA to list your ingredients by order of weight or volume. If you spent 10 percent of your time answering the phones in your last office job and you are applying for a job as a receptionist, you had better list phones first and go on to typing and filing later. You know the "ingredients rule" for resumes: **Put your information in order of interest to the targeted reader.**

Focus your past to relate to your future. Just changing the order of your sentences, *without changing a single word,* will change the impact and focus of your resume. Of course, most of the time you'll want to change the order and some of the wording every time you refocus your document.

For example, look at these two very different ways to present the exact same job:

A secretary seeking a job as a receptionist:

Mutual Benevolent of Omaha, Omaha, Nebraska   2008–2010
Secretary (Receptionist), Marketing Department

- Screened all incoming calls and visitors.

- Maintained knowledge of location/work status of all executives in the marketing department.

- Controlled flow of information into/out of the department.

- Projected a professional image for the department at all times.

- Also provided general office support as needed.

The same secretary seeking a job as executive assistant:

Mutual Benevolent of Omaha, Omaha, Nebraska   2008–2010
Secretary (Assistant to the V.P. Marketing), Marketing Department

- Provided office and administrative support to the V.P. Marketing and other executives in the marketing department.

- Prepared documents for release, including letters, memos, and product information. Drafted official correspondence for signature by the V.P. Marketing.

- Prepared complex travel itineraries for executives and marketing teams.

- Also served as front desk/receptionist for the department.

Repeat this ranking and selecting process for all information you present, going back roughly ten to fifteen years of work history. Remember to pay attention to design as you transfer this information onto your rough draft. **You are well on your way to a dynamic resume.**

To assist you, here are few sample experience listings. Your listings do not need to be as long as some of these to be effective, but do not make them so short they do not stick in the mind. And remember:

- Don't be boring.

- Throw out the obvious.

- Start each sentence with an action verb.

- Search for the superlative!

- Quantify everything.
- Be precise.

Samples

Too Big to Fail Bank, NT & SA, New York, New York

Manager, Wholesale Receivables   2008–2010

Directed billing and collections for $100,000,000 in corporate fee receivables from the bank's largest clients (all Fortune 500). Staff of six.

- Developed software QA program to track productivity individually and departmentwide. Successfully reduced staff by 50 percent with concurrent increase in productivity.

- Recovered $243,000 in unbilled fees in internal audit; created database and new operating procedures to prevent future underbilling problems.

- Co-designed application to track LBO fees to comply with FASB regulations.

Manager, Bank Secrecy Compliance   2005–2007

Recruited by the S.V.P. to design bankwide policies and procedures to achieve compliance with federal Bank Secrecy Act and constantly evolving rules and regulations governing data security.

- Analyzed information flow and databanking resources bankwide. Developed and implemented policies, procedures, and training programs.

- Reduced and streamlined data flow, eliminated duplicate entry systems, saving $389,000 in the first year and annually thereafter.

- Reduced error rate from 78 percent of manual entries to 2 percent in six-month period.

- Developed supporting research proving improvement, resulting in 87.5 percent reduction of multimillion-dollar fine from IRS.

SAN DIEGO YACHT CLUB, San Diego, California, Summer 2010
Lead Instructor

- Organized and managed summer Junior Sailing Program serving 180 students, aged 8 to 18.

- Trained and supervised 10 instructors.

- Reported to the SDYC Board of Directors.

Restaurant Management Systems, Inc., Detroit, Michigan   2010–Present
Unit Manager, Chicago

- Manage all aspects of high-volume corporate-owned restaurant (Baldwin & Bonds). Full P&L responsibility, reporting to the chain manager. Strong performance as interim manager and floating troubleshooter led to assignment as GM of this flagship unit, the largest and most profitable in the chain. Consistently exceed objectives for gross, net, and share.

- Hire, train, motivate staff of 64. Have gained the trust and support of personnel working in a multicultural, multiracial, multilingual environment. Enjoy high staff morale and lowest turnover in the chain. Personally committed to production of a top-quality product in a clean, sanitary, and attractive environment.

Selected accomplishments:

- Achieved 17.25 percent volume increase and 15.9 percent profit increase in first assignment as interim unit manager. Promoted to top volume unit (Chicago).

- Achieved 22.05 percent volume increase and 19.0 percent profit increase. Earned Top Manager award. Earned two QSC awards (Quality, Service, Cleanliness).

- Earned Top Ten dinner with the president (top 10 percent nationwide).

———————

APEX, ZENITH & ACME, MANAGEMENT CONSULTANTS

Boston, Massachusetts   2010–Present

Executive Assistant to the CEO

Manage CEO's calendar, daily schedule, and extensive travel arrangements. Represent the CEO within the organization, to our 75 affiliated management consulting firms, and directly to clients. Control information flow into and out of the executive suite. Plan and coordinate meetings, conferences, and other events nationwide. Solve problems as they arise. Ensure CEO has all information and resources required for maximum efficiency.

- Hand-picked for this position by the CEO. Have achieved his complete respect and trust. *Excellent recommendation available.*

- Increased flow of information between CEO, officers, and the 75 affiliates. CEO increased travel commitments *and* increased day-to-day control over this diversified company.

- Facilitated development of new five-year strategic business plan, by orchestrating deliverables of related studies and research projects (completed ahead of schedule).

- Developed and implemented a "real time" commitment tracking system to record, track, and control the CEO's obligations moment-by-moment.

- Due to increase in efficiency in CEO's offices, was able to eliminate one position through attrition, resulting in savings in excess of $80,000 per annum.

———————

Engineers and Consultants

There is a variation on the above style used by engineers and consultants, and that is to list projects as accomplishments. Consultants and engineers will give a scope statement covering the type of responsibilities they normally assume; then they will describe projects or engagements.

Here are two examples:

Holman-Johnston, Engineers   Houston, Texas

   Director of Field Operations and Civil/Structural Engineer   2008–Present

   Holman-Johnston is a global engineering company with annual revenues of US $16 million, world leader in design-build of offshore structures, including traditional steel platforms and experimental designs.

   Field engineering manager in charge of offshore platform installation projects. Project planning, global logistics, offshore fabrication, local labor and vendor selection, client liaison. Typically in charge of approximately 50 site personnel.

Sample projects:

   Field Engineer, Jolliet TLWP floating platform for Chevron, installed in 1712 feet of water in the Gulf of Mexico. This was a first-of-its-kind installation. Supervised and coordinated 60 welders, riggers, divers, surveyors, tugboat captains, and marine crane operators. Developed classes and trained foremen, engineers, winch drivers, mates, and others every day for two weeks, before installation of never-before-tried engineering plans.

   Company Representative, Gulf Marine Fabricators, Aransas Pass, Texas. Verified compliance with design provided by our engineering department. Updated scheduling and field progress reports with home office. Modified rigging layout, reducing costs by 8 percent on over 1 mile of heavy installation. Supervised during jacket load out (24,000 tons).

   Field Engineer and Construction Supervisor, British Petroleum, North Sea. Supervised launch and pile barges for ULA platforms, in charge of 80 welders, riggers, foremen, and inspectors under extremely harsh weather conditions.

   Also had office engineering management and planning assignments in between field projects (20 percent of duty time).

Linda C. Akizarny dba **Marketing Design Group**   2009–Present
Philadelphia, Pennsylvania

   Marketing Consultant

   Initiated, structured, and conducted marketing consulting projects, including all phases of business analysis, market analysis, demographic analysis, site selection, image development, and media planning.

Sample engagements:

- **NEW FACES, EDUCATION DIVISION** Provided start-up marketing plans for a cosmetic surgery cooperative based in New England. Worked directly with the founder of the cooperative to develop realistic marketing budgets and plans for various business launch scenarios. Ongoing.

- **EASTERN COLLEGE OF APPLIED TECHNOLOGY** Revamped marketing and advertising functions for this for-profit educational enterprise with 15 campuses. Restructured $4 million annual combined advertising/marketing budget. Achieved 41 percent increase in applications with no increase in budget. 2010.

- **PAPYRUS, INC.** Retained to establish structure and internal marketing function for newly formed franchise department of an aggressive, rapid-growth retail chain. Provided competitive analysis (SWOT), collaborated on business plan development and strategic plan for nationwide franchise rollout. 2009.

By the way, if you are tempted to list consulting to cover a period of unemployment, you will need to list actual, verifiable engagements like the ones above to achieve any credibility at all. Remember, anything you say in your resume can and will be tested in an interview, so never make up experiences that didn't happen as they are described.

10 Writing Your Resume: What to Do about Common Problems

Unrelated Experience

Whenever I give a lecture, somebody always asks me some version of "What do I do with unrelated jobs?" Either make them relevant, or move them to a less prominent area in the resume. You can also just leave them out entirely. Use the resume "ingredients rule" and your own creativity to demonstrate how the experience would support your next job objective.

If your most important jobs fall behind unimportant or unimpressive jobs, consider regrouping your jobs under subheadings, such as "RELATED EXPERIENCE" and "ADDITIONAL EXPERIENCE," or "MANAGEMENT EXPERIENCE" and "SALES EXPERIENCE." You can also just reorder your jobs altogether. Consider listing your jobs out of chronological order. Put them **in order of interest to your targeted reader.** Keep the dates accurate, or remove them altogether (see below). It's unorthodox, but sometimes unorthodox presentations open doors.

You may be able to describe seemingly unrelated experience in a way that supports your latest job goal. The following listing shows a restaurant worker's intelligence, sales skill, and business savvy:

Neptune's Sea Palace, Miami, Florida   2010–Present
   Food Server

> Act as a "sales representative" for the restaurant, selling add-ons and extras to achieve one of the highest per-ticket and per-night sales averages. Prioritize and juggle dozens of simultaneous responsibilities. Have built loyal clientele of regulars, in addition to tourist trade. Fully computerized environment.

The next listing shows how a menial job at a letter-sorting machine can be used to support a candidacy for beginning systems analyst. The resume reader may not know what an L.S.M. is, but you can be sure that he will be favorably impressed by this job listing:

U.S.P.S. (United States Postal Service)   2009–2010
L.S.M. Operator

> Worked average of 50–60 hours per week while full-time student, demonstrating work ethic, endurance, and sustained efficiency. Comfortable with large volume of responsibility. Excellent accuracy under deadline and in fast-paced work environment.

The prior listing illustrates a very good point about resumes: Your reader does not have to understand exactly what you have written, or exactly what you have done, as long as every possible interpretation is positive. Never be vague by accident; be vague on purpose.

No Experience

Another common question is "What do I do if I have no valuable work history at all?" Whenever this question comes up, I think of a woman who walked into my first career consulting office, many years ago. She told me that she had never had a job, she had never even worked, and while we were on the subject, she couldn't do anything anyway.

As I was interviewing her in preparation for some serious creative writing, I discovered that she had been the bookkeeper for her husband's business for ten years. Her husband ran a floating fish-processing factory in Alaska, a "seasonal business" she called it. How big? "About $3.5 million dollars, more or less, depending on the season. And I guess I do manage our rental properties while he's gone every year." What did that entail? "Well, I buy property, fix it up, and rent it out." It turned out she was in total charge of the properties, a multimillion-dollar portfolio back when that was a lot of money.

Your case will be different, but I think you get the point. Think. You are bound to have some valuable history. Remember to consider your part-time, temporary, avocational, or philanthropic experiences.

If you honestly lack valuable or related experience, **get some.** Volunteer, take a class, take a lower-level position to gain exposure. Demonstrate and substantiate your interest in your career objective. I had a client who had tried unsuccessfully for over two years to get into city planning. I encouraged him to sign up for some classes. He did, and we listed on his resume that he was an *enrollee* in a city planning program. With his new resume, demonstrating his *intention* to take some classes, he got a job in city planning before the first class even started. To his credit, he continued the program and eventually got his master's degree.

I had another client who thought he could be sales manager at an auto dealership after running a video rental store. That's just dumb. He thought he could skip selling cars and jump to the second highest position in an auto dealership. Be realistic about your entry point, especially when switching industries.

Recent college graduates can always opt for a post-baccalaureate internship, or they can get more mileage out of their college experiences (see below).

Military Experience

What do you do with military experience? Treat it exactly like any other kind of experience. As mentioned earlier, translate all the jargon into standard business terms. Stress the leadership and management aspects of your service, and you get extra points if you can work in common business terms such as *budgets, ROI,* and *customer service.* There's more about this on page 8.

If your military service was long ago, or not so relevant to your current duties, you can list it at the bottom of your resume, in a short listing:

MILITARY
> **Colonel (ret.), United States Marine Corps**
>
> Bronze Star, Purple Heart (2)

College Experiences

College students can make particular use of student activities, informal experience, and classroom projects to show their skills and abilities. Here are three examples:

Black Student Union, Midland University   Midland Delta, Mississippi
> **President**   2009–2010
>
> Provided leadership to a student organization representing 22 percent of the total student body. Liaison to university administration. Member, Minority Student Affairs Board.

Selected contributions:

- Improved the image and the relevancy of the organization campus wide.

- Increased budget by 40 percent and membership by over 100 percent.

- Obtained changes in the university's hiring policies to increase diversity of professoriate.

- Organized the first-ever All South Scholars of Color Student Affairs Conference, 2010.

Senior Design Studio Senior Project
> **International Media Group.** (IBD Student Competition.) Developed design for 9th floor of Moffett Building (100 Bush, San Francisco). Provided design concept, space plan, finishes, presentation boards, floor/ceiling plans, reception desk, and model.

University of Wisconsin, Madison   2009–2010
> **Research Associate,** Chemistry Department

Conducted experiments in strict accordance with written methodologies to originate data used in Prof. Pritchard's articles published in the *Journal of the American Chemical Society (JACS)*. Additional details on request.

For more on student resumes, see the next chapter, "Education and Additional Data." Also see resume samples on pages 65–66, 69, 79–81, 91, and 93.

Self-Employed

What do you do if you are self-employed? Employers have justified fears of the self-employed. The two main fears are that you are too independent to take orders and fit into an organizational structure, and that you will learn their business and go into competition against them. Pretty scary fears, right? Do yourself a favor. Downplay self-employment as much as possible. Decide if you can call yourself "manager" or "director of business development" instead of "owner" or "founder." Do not call the company "Albert Bernard Chasworth, Inc.," call it "ABC, Inc." There are exceptions, of course, but a word to the wise is sufficient. Once you are in the interview, reveal all. This type of technique is valid to get into an interview, but it is a mistake to carry it too far.

I once used a similar technique to solve the problem for an exotic dancer who wanted to go into something new. We wrote it up, briefly, this way:

QSMC, Miami, Florida   2008–2010
   Hostess and **Customer Service Representative**

No need to call attention to the fact she was working at Queen of Sheba Men's Club.

Gaps in Dates

What do you do about job gaps? This is a really good question. There are many good reasons for job gaps, and it is perfectly acceptable to have a gap somewhere in your career as long as you can explain it in an interview. My suggestion is simple: Show the gap without comment and be prepared to discuss it in an interview or telephone inquiry from the hiring authority.

Do not fill in the missing time on your resume with some excusatory line like, "2006–2009, family obligations" or "2006–2009, prison." Such a line does not support your candidacy in any way. Be sure you do not fall for the temptation to "adjust" dates from legitimate experience to cover gaps. Fudging on your dates is very dangerous, and the risk is simply not proportional to the gain. See resume writing rule #4: **Never, never, tell a lie.**

There are several ways to obscure and deemphasize dates, the chief of which is to list dates by year only. The real point is that contemporary employers are not fixated on continuous employment. Most workers have gaps in their employment now. I am in favor of de-emphasizing dates on general principle. Dates do not of themselves demonstrate a job skill or talent.

What if you have not worked in over a year? This is another date question. One of my favorite techniques for this is to take a reading like "2007–2008" and let it read open-ended, "2007–" as though you meant "2007–Present." This is called the tombstone technique. In resumes, curiosity will almost always work in your favor. Here is how this might look:

Jorgensen & Daughters General Contractors   2007–
    Project Manager

Another date technique is to list experience as "current" and "prior" without specifying any dates at all. Avoid using duration, such as "two years" or "six years," where you would have put the actual dates. This is distracting and raises far more questions than it answers.

It is okay to leave dates out entirely, but you will face some suspicion if you do. This suspicion, however, is often an easier liability to overcome than the liability revealed by the dates themselves. Some of the resume samples in chapters 13 and 14 have omitted or purposely obfuscated the dates, all without telling a lie. See the resume for Dean Rodgers on page 68, for Pi Qi Ling on page 71, and for Chrystal Ann Horton on page 90.

Prisoners and Parents

It is fascinating to me that prisoners returning to society and stay-at-home parents returning to work face almost identical career and resume problems. Both categories of workers have old experience that may be important but little or no recent experience. Both may be out of date on technology, and both may lack the networks that people commonly use to find employment.

Although stay-at-home moms and dads always have the option of staying mum on why they've been out of the job market, prisoners are often *required* to reveal that they are on probation or in work release programs. That's the main difference.

Those returning to the workforce can use the techniques above to manage gaps in dates. Prisoners and parents may need to start well below their potential in order to gain a foothold in the job market. *Rapid career advancement achieved by a series of promotions or job changes* is often the only way for a prisoner or returning parent to get back to their full potential in the job market. This is really a career problem more than a resume problem per se.

Anyone returning to the job market will have to show that they are up to date. They may need to take some classes on the latest technologies at the local community college. They may need to build a web site, start a noncontroversial blog, twitter about their job search experience, and so on, to show they're not behind the curve.

Overqualified

If you are angling for a position below the level of your most recent assignment, you will need to translate your experiences down so that you don't scare off a potential employer. Instead of saying you "set strategy for the sales effort" you say you did something much more mundane, such as "wrote scripts for training new sales staff." Instead of saying you "supervised a total staff of 64," suddenly you say you "supervised staff." Remember, never be vague by accident; be vague on purpose.

Be wary of changing your title. If your title is "Group Vice President," that's what your title is. You can make your title disappear by naming your department or division instead, or your function. It's pretty tricky, right on the edge of acceptable practice, but it's worked for some of my clients in the past.

Once in the interview, you'll have to work hard to sell the fact that you'll be excited about this opportunity, you'll stay long enough to create real value, and you won't act like you're slumming among the lesser people by deigning to work there at all. Those are interview issues, however, not resume problems.

Here're two examples, showing how to translate down an experience:

BIG DEAL TECHCO, Peoria, Illinois
Sales Manager
Directed sales and new business development strategy for the company. Reported to the founder and CEO. Collaborated with him on roll out of new product lines, including advising on commercialization of the firm's technologies. Identified target sectors for new product lines, and increased sales of existing products on the market. Trained and motivated an industrial sales team of 6 field professionals and in-office sales support team of 23. Created 325% growth rate.

BIG DEAL TECHCO, Peoria, Illinois
Sales
Sold technology products to national accounts. Identified and accessed decision-makers at the C level (CIO, CTO, CFO, COO). Consistently had one of the highest closing ratios in the company. Major contributor to 325% growth rate at this company.

Also, consider dropping that M.B.A. or Ph.D. if it doesn't fit with your newly positioned job history. In a tight economy, and especially if you can't relocate, taking a step down is much smarter than suffering long-term unemployment.

Job Hoppers

What do you do about too many jobs, too many cities, and so on? It should be obvious by now: If you have too many jobs, omit some. If every job is in a new city, omit *all* the cities. Look at the following two chronologies, the same work history presented in very different ways:

Truck Driver, XYZ Industrial Plant, Louisville, Kentucky	9/2010–Present
Fire Fighter, U.S. Bureau of Lumber & Mines, Wenatchee, Washington	6/2010–9/2010
Delivery Driver, Sno-Frost Cake & Candy, Dallas, Texas	12/2009–1/2010

Welder's Assistant, Firefly Oil Field Supply, Grand Isle, Louisiana   6/2009–8/2009

Forklift Driver, Empire Building Supply, Ithaca, New York   6/2008–3/2009

Bartender, Hemingway's, Key West, Florida   4/2008–6/2008

Tow Truck Driver, Able Tow & Wreck, Winnemucca, Nevada   12/2006–1/2008

What do you think of this candidate? Unreliable, a "road scholar." Now look what happens if you take an eraser to this background:

Truck Driver, XYZ Industrial Plant   2010–Present

Delivery Driver, Sno-Frost Cake & Candy   2009–2010

Forklift Driver, Empire Building Supply   2008–2009

Tow Truck Driver, Able Tow & Wreck   2006–2008

This is still quite a few jobs, but I see a definite career path and, for a driver, reasonable duration. Tell me this candidate has a clean driving record, no tickets, and no accidents in the last seven years, and I may be interested.

Sometimes the best thing you can do with some of your information is leave it out.

Perhaps by now you are getting a feel for the approach to solving resume problems. Do not learn a handful of tricks from this book. Learn a way of thinking. Then you can solve your own problem, no matter how unusual it may be.

11 Writing Your Resume: Education and Additional Data

If your career has progressed logically and is well represented by your experience, your education can be rather briefly stated, with or without dates:

M.B.A., Howard University, Washington, D.C.

B.S., Economics, Duke University, Durham, North Carolina

The following education listings cover most typical cases. Some are a little more creative than others, but all are common and accepted practice.

B.S.B.A. (Bachelor of Science in Business Administration), ongoing
Arizona State University, Tempe

―――――――――

M.D., Harvard Medical School, Boston, Massachusetts, 2008

B.A., Biology, Reed College, Portland, Oregon, 2004

―――――――――

B.A., Marketing, S.U.N.Y., Buffalo, expected 2013

―――――――――

M.S.S.W. (Master of Science Program in Social Work), enrollee
University of Texas, Arlington

―――――――――

B.A. (Bachelor of Arts in Psychology), 2009
University of Illinois, Urbana-Champagne

Ph.D. (ABD), Anthropology, 2010
B.S., Anthropology, *magna cum laude,* 2006
University of California, Berkeley

"ABD" stands for "all but dissertation." Similarly, "ABT" stands for "all but thesis." These are two of the handiest abbreviations in higher education.

If you abandoned an advanced degree program, don't apologize for it. Do not write "M.B.A. Candidate, 2002–2003." Instead, turn it into a positive statement, as in the following:

Golden Gate University, San Francisco, California
Graduate Studies in Finance and Business Analysis, 2002–2003

If you have a B.A. in music history and you are now an accountant, you may wish to list your undergraduate degree without specifying a major:

B.A., Boston University, Boston, Massachusetts

If you went to school but did not graduate, do not claim a degree. Anybody can call any registrar's office in America and say, "I'm calling to verify a degree," and less than sixty seconds later they will know the truth of the matter. (Incidentally, if you hire people, make it a point to check.) If you took even one college course, you can use a listing like the following:

Psychology, Tulane University, New Orleans, Louisiana

That won't satisfy every screener, but if you have relevant experience and manage your job search well, you will definitely receive consideration from the majority of employers and you *will* get a good job. Accept your shortcomings, *whatever they may be.* Your education will only be a stumbling block if you let it be one.

If your education is truly nonexistent, then omit it. I have had only one professional candidate in my executive coaching career who did not have any college education at all—not one day in a college classroom, not one management seminar, nothing. He had dropped out of high school to become a super-roadie, designing one-of-a-kind audio equipment and high-tech visual effects for alternative rock bands, and after several career twists, he had become a process automation engineer.

So we left education off entirely. He had a very impressive two-page resume, which was handy because whichever page the reader was on, he could assume the education was on the other. It worked. My client was flown across the continent for interviews with an exciting robotics engineering firm. They even negotiated an offer before the matter finally came up. When it did come up, my candidate was ready: "All my life I have been working on newly-emerging technology and, frankly, I just couldn't take the time out to go to school to study science that was obsolete."

He got the job.

Whatever your limitations may be, accept them and go on. Get out there and sell yourself on your strengths.

After you have a good job, then really think about getting that degree. No matter how old you are, you will not get any younger, and to paraphrase Dear Abby, how old will you be in X years if you don't get that degree now? Also, as people change jobs more frequently, it is a nuisance to have to run this gauntlet over and over again.

Even if you have one degree, if you are under thirty-five, you had better seriously think about an advanced degree soon. Your career may be an exception, but I am seeing more and more careers choked off because of the lack of an M.B.A. or other advanced education. This is particularly true in the fast lane of business, but also in any lane of education, social services, science, engineering, and even in such unlikely fields as government and the military. Not everyone wants more and more career challenges, but if you do, take a hard look at your credentials. Also, if you decide to apply to a graduate program, take advantage of my book, *Graduate Admissions Essays*, the best-selling guide to getting into graduate school.

Recent college graduates can make a big presentation out of their education section. It can include classes, honors, awards, activities, affiliations, study abroad, special projects, their GPA, their golf handicap, and practically anything you can imagine. If recent education is one of your greatest qualifications for a position, feel free to feature items like these:

University of Nevada, Las Vegas, Nevada
Bachelor of Science in Hotel Administration, expected May 2012
> Dean's Honors
> St. Tropez Partnership Scholar
> Eta Sigma Delta International Hospitality Honor Society (Vice President)
> Professional Convention Management Association
> Hospitality Association (Golf Team)
> Intramural Squash (Champions)

Everything from athletics to tutoring can be listed. One thing to be careful about, however, is how you present a nonacademic sorority or fraternity. If you were president, vice president, or treasurer, feature your leadership role and contributions. Admitting that you chaired the social committee, on the other hand, is tantamount to admitting that you are an expert at drinking beer. In fact, not only are you an expert at this important and arcane skill, but you teach this skill to others. Show a little wisdom and emphasize any community service projects.

The most compelling college-related listings will be actual classes taken. Use the word "coursework" so you can paraphrase class titles instead of being bound by the official title.

Michigan State University
B.S., Business Administration

Coursework included:

Accounting I & II	Marketing Strategy & Planning
Sales and Sales Management	Statistics I & II
Corporate Finance	Marketing Research

Computer and Tech Skills:

HTML Programming & Web Page Design	Spreadsheet Design
PowerPoint (Super User)	Database Design

This technique is particularly useful for featuring classes you may have taken outside your major, if they support your current job objective.

Should You List High School?

Finally, if you have no college experience and want to list a high school diploma, even that can be spiced up:

Diploma, College Preparatory Studies, 2008
Central High School, Middletown, Ohio

- High Scores in Math and Science
- "Athletic Scholar" Award for Simultaneous Letter and Honor Roll

In the Northeast, it is common to list prep schools on resumes, particularly in certain industries such as finance. West of the Atlantic Seaboard I would probably recommend against it. In much of the U.S., "Phillips Exeter" might sound more like a tobacco product than an elite academy.

Some foreign nationals who went to high school in the U.S. or Canada will list it to show the depth of their connection to North America, with an implied deeper command of English.

So follow the resume ingredients rule. Feature the information that sells you. If your education is overwhelming or some of it is irrelevant, you can move some of it to near the bottom of your resume under a heading such as "ADDITIONAL EDUCATION & TRAINING." I actually saw a candidate from Florida with this listing at the bottom of his resume: "HOBBIES: Ph.D., Astrophysics."

Write your education section now.

Then, as you proceed through the following sections, add in pertinent data or additional headings if you need to.

Using a "SPECIAL PROJECTS" Heading

If education is one of your only qualifications for your next position, you may also choose to pull out special projects and make them listings unto themselves. These listings can include a mix of class work, projects from co-op or internships, or even projects you just did on your own out of special interest. Here is an example:

SPECIAL PROJECTS:

Interior Architecture

- Designed high-volume Thai restaurant kitchen, including visiting Thai restaurants and interviewing Thai chefs on cooking techniques and layout. Specified and costed out all equipment, designed utility conduits, consulted on OSHA and California-state requirements and regulations. A senior class honors project. Earned "Top Design Project 2010" award.

- Designed tenant improvements for a 1200 s.f. minimalist concept clothing store. Visited minimalist stores in Manhattan and on Rodeo Drive. Took design from as-built measurements of a real space in Beverly Hills to client presentation portfolio with schematics and drawings.

Residential Design

- Designed a writer's bungalow/pool house for a professional screenwriter in Santa Monica. Researched soundproofing technologies; designed 1100 s.f. multiuse building.

Also see the resume on page 79 for another example.

Professional Credentials and Licenses

Professional credentials can be cited either at the top of the resume—in the profile or in their own section—or near the bottom with the education section or in their own category. Do not assume that your reader will realize you have professional credentials because you have a job that requires them. They should to be explicitly stated.

C.P.A., State of California, since 2001
Member, State Bar of New York, admitted 2007
NASD Series 7 License, current

Credentials can be listed as "pending" if you are writing your resume after you have sat for the exam, and before the results are released.

Languages

The business world is increasingly international. If you are even remotely likely to use a language skill in your next job, list it either in your profile, if it is highly relevant, or under your education or in a heading by itself if it is less obviously relevant. Remember, the more important the skill is the more likely it belongs in your profile. So if the job requires travel to France, your French language skills need to be featured at the top of the resume; if there is no obvious need for francophone skills, then such skills can be relegated to a lower section.

Language skills can be defined: bilingual, fluent, proficient, intermediate, basic. Don't forget that if you write "bilingual/bicultural in Mandarin" someone searching for "fluent in Chinese" *will miss you entirely.* So, find a way to put all the various search terms someone may use into your resume, even if the writing becomes less than elegant. "LANGUAGES: Chinese (Mandarin), bilingual/bicultural, fully fluent in Chinese, able to interpret and translate into/out of English and Chinese, including technical information." That's a clunker of a sentence, but it covers all the bases.

Affiliations, Community Service, Hobbies, Clubs, Personal Pursuits

As a general rule, these categories strengthen a weak candidate and weaken a strong candidate. In any case, the most *directly related* and *candidacy-supporting* organizations should be listed.

For example, if you are interested in a position in import/export, belonging to the World Trade Club might be seen as a plus. If you are an import/export executive, it would be even better if you were an officer of the organization or a featured speaker. But your participation in the Neighborhood Watch Program is trivial and distracting.

For 99.44 percent of people reading this sentence, listing hobbies on your resume will be fluff. Once again, only the most *directly related* and *candidacy-supporting* hobbies should be listed. In all my years of writing resumes, I can only think of one instance that exemplifies a directly related and candidacy-supporting hobby. This particular computer science jobseeker was a real Rube Goldberg, with a house full of electro-mechanical equipment and a passion for designing robots. He had robots to vacuum the floor, fetch coffee, retrieve the newspaper, chase the kids, you name it. If your hobby is not this strongly related to your objective, I would leave it out.

Another use for this section is to reveal aspects of your identity. If you wish to reveal that you are gay, or African American, or Azerbaijani, here is one place to do it. There is no doubt that membership in the Azerbaijani Students Association identifies you as Azerbaijani.

I used to think that such identifications had no place on a resume, ever, but my point of view is changing. I tried to take an organization off a gentleman's resume because it identified him as gay. He was very clear about why he wanted it put back: "I don't care to work in an office that is homophobic."

Although I can understand this sentiment, it is still my professional opinion that any information that can play to an employer's base prejudices, against or for the candidate, should be avoided. Your ability to perform your duties should be the focus of your resume, not your status as a former model, a minority, or member of a particular church.

Get the interview based on your job skills, as clearly presented on your resume. Then use your professionalism, personality, and the strength of your qualifications to overcome any unfair and irrelevant prejudices your employer may have. If you do a good job of answering the question, "What can this candidate do for me?" your potential employer is not going to care if you have tattoos or if you are a green Martian.

Be careful of using this section to make a statement about your personality, politics, or lifestyle. Yoga may be a life-enriching activity for you, but mentioning it may make you seem flaky to your potential employer. Your status as a deacon in a Baptist church may be a negative factor to someone who is Jewish or Roman Catholic. Even your sports activities may be an unconscious turnoff to the tired, cigarette-smoking vice president who reads your resume at 9 P.M.

These types of information have their own name in resume jargon: throw-out factors. They are irrelevant or personal data that do little or nothing to advance your candidacy, yet create a potential for your resume to be thrown out. In business terms, the possible upside is small, the possible downside is terminal.

If you are way older than all the other candidates, listing your time in a recent marathon may have some value. If you really plan to entertain clients on the links, then maybe you should mention your golf talents. However, the general rule is: **Unless you plan to do it on your job, leave it out.**

Personal Section

If you are not a native citizen or are likely to be misidentified as such, I recommend that you specify your work status: Under a "PERSONAL" section, state that you are a "Resident Alien, valid 'Green Card,' qualified for immediate employment," or "U.S. citizen since 2002," or "Canadian citizen since 1998," and so on. Also, as mentioned before, listing graduation from an American high school can address this issue.

Additional

You can put a grab bag heading such as this near the bottom of your resume. This section can contain foreign-language skills, relevant travel experiences, availability, and any loose items that you feel are important to convey to a potential employer. I try to avoid needing to write a section like this, but it is common enough to have one.

Think over your whole background. Is there some skill or credential that is tangential enough to be distracting in your profile, but potentially important enough to include near the bottom of your presentation? If so, add it now.

There is a resume-writing theory that says you should end your resume with one last punch, which may fall under an "ADDITIONAL" heading, but I can't really endorse it. Your resume should have its punch at the top and wind down toward the end. I certainly would not wait until this section to introduce critical information. If your qualifications are less than perfect, however, you may wish to throw a few final hooks in the end, to try to stay in the "yes" pile.
Examples:

Proven performer with a desire to tackle a new challenge. Comfortable with high-end, sophisticated, conceptual, and/or technical products. Available for unlimited travel as needed.

Aspiring writer with the talent and the desire to succeed. Proven performer in extremely competitive environments. Self-directed, highly energetic. Completed bachelor of arts degree in three-and-a-half years while working full time. Committed to the pursuit of excellence in work and lifelong learning.

What *not* to Include

In an American resume, you should never list your height, weight, physical condition, age or date of birth, marital status, number/names/ages of your kids, salary, reason for leaving a position, street addresses for employers, social security number, driver's license number, or similar personal data. You immediately identify yourself as a "resume dinosaur" who has not read a resume book since 1978. This is not funny. Your potential employer will assume that all of your management ideas are from 1978, too.

International Resumes or CVs Are the Exception

"C.V." or "CV" stands for curriculum vitae. That is a style of resume used in Europe and Asia and, really, everywhere outside of North America. (In the U.S. and Canada, a CV is an academic style of resume, which is covered in chapter 14, "Special Styles, More Solutions." In short, CVs list education first, never have an objective, and have a very brief style for employment listings.) If you are applying for work internationally, you should know that the entire rest of the world lists date of birth and marital status, at least. (In Japan, employers want to know which grammar school you attended, so they can discern the neighborhood you grew up in, and presumably, what kind of a person you are.)

If you send your resume overseas, it is okay to include such personal data, but certainly not height and weight. The following listing was designed to allow the client to use his resume anywhere in the world.

> **PERSONAL:**
> Available for travel and offshore assignments anywhere in the world.
> Date of birth: February 2, 1980.
> Citizenship: United Kingdom. Passport: United Kingdom.
> Married to U.S. Citizen. Status: U.S. Resident Alien, valid "Green Card."
> Qualified to work throughout the U.S. and E.U., without reservations.
> References and additional details provided on interview.

There are many styles of CVs, and regional differences are important. If you are interested, read Mary Anne Thompson's books, or visit www.goinglobal.com.

References

Do not list your references on your resume, no matter who they are. References, portfolios, bibliographies, transcripts, writing samples, and the like can all be offered on request. As a general rule, you can forego the rote statement "References on request." This is understood. If you're not going to put some twist on the line, it's best just to leave it out. A sample reference list is on page 126.

Some people end their resumes with a cautionary note: "References gladly provided upon request, but please keep this application confidential at this time." This might be particularly pertinent if your current employer is happy with your work and doesn't know you are looking for a new job.

That is not a bad image to leave a prospective employer with, anyway: that you're valued where you are now. If you really want to protect yourself from indiscreet recruiters, make your application anonymous! Look again at the advice on page 20 on how to use names and contact info that cannot be traced back to you.

Key Words List

This is a really big secret, so don't tell anybody: Smart resume writers are placing "KEYWORDS LIST" categories at or near the end of their resumes, especially resumes used online. In this section they throw in every word the employer might *ever* search for that would be related to a job they might want. Because it is a keywords list, there is no context for the word. You are not necessarily representing that you have the skill or experience, just that the words are related to your interests. To be plain, this beats resume-sorting software.

You need humans to read your resume to get a job. Because job boards have millions of candidates listed, employers use keywords to find people with a high likelihood of being interested in and appropriate for a job. If a human reads your resume, they can overlook a "requirement" or two, if they like everything else about you. Recruiters don't like you to outsmart their software, but my allegiance is to you. A keyword list is a great technique. Don't be abusive, but understand the power of this recommendation. They can't like you if they don't talk to you.

Some people have made sport of the fact that words printed in any size font the same color as the background are invisible. They won't be invisible to a computer, and that's the point. I really can't endorse using invisible writing, however, as the words won't remain invisible if a recruiter takes your resume and converts it to a new format (which is common). So I wouldn't use this technique. The keywords list accomplishes the same goal, without duplicity.

Congratulations! The first draft of your resume is done.

12 Writing Your Resume: Putting It All Together

How Does It Feel?

Take a long look at the first draft of your resume. How does it look? How do you feel?

Most of us find the act of putting together a resume exhilarating, even cathartic. Seldom in life do we sit back and really take account of our accomplishments. In a thousand ways, every one of us is an unsung hero. This is one chance we have to sing that song. Take a moment to savor it.

———————

Now look again. *Think*. Did you leave anything out? If you did, stop now and put it in. Do not worry about how long your resume is. We will address that in a few seconds. When you are satisfied that everything that needs to be in your resume is in it, only then will we proceed to take things out.

Final Edit

There are some norms about length. A college student or graduate is supposed to have a one-page version of her resume, even if she also has a two-page version. An MBA student or new graduate is supposed to have a one-page version, as well. Finance and Wall Street resumes tend to be one page, even for people earning seven figures. Many hiring managers in IT and engineering report a strong bias in favor of one-page resumes. Otherwise, my suggestion is: Write it until it's done. For most regular careerists with significant experience, a two-page or even three-page resume is acceptable, especially if it has an effective profile and it reads well. Executives can and do have three- and four-page versions, sometimes more. Frankly, a skilled designer can make a resume longer or shorter, without changing a word.

Look at your resume. Would it be stronger if it were a little shorter? There are several techniques to shorten, strengthen, and improve your presentation. To put it simply: Throw things out or summarize them.

Ernest Hemingway called his eraser a "shit detector." Take a look at your sentences. How many adjectives can be thrown out? How many statements will be obvious to your intended reader? Check your resume for tone. Be especially wary of sounding pompous. "Excellent" and "outstanding," when applied to oneself, can have an unintended effect on the reader.

Your resume should wind down toward the end. As a general rule, each job listing should be a little shorter than the last. Give your recent experience full exposure, but as you get back to ten or fifteen years ago, just stop. This has a very interesting effect. If you remove dates from your education, it is impossible to date you. You cannot be discriminated against because of your age, whatever it is, since your age is not available.

Employers have a profile in mind of the candidate they are looking for. That profile can be very specific. This is not really a form of prejudice—though it can work out that way—just standard management planning. The best managers think visually, they project the future visually, and you may not be in that vision. So revealing data that can be counted against you, *even subconsciously,* is something you should avoid. Once you are in the interview, you can easily demonstrate why you are the right person for the job, even if you were not the candidate they had previewed in their mind. Do not let subconscious prejudices keep you from getting an interview. Keep throw-out factors out of your resume.

Besides, few banking vice presidents are stronger candidates because of a full delineation of their duties as a "Vault Teller" early in their career. If you have older experience that you feel supports your candidacy, use an encompassing statement without dates:

PRIOR:
Executive Assistant to the CEO, Ajax & MacDonald Machine Tool Co., Akron, Ohio
Office Manager, Dewey, Cheatham, and Howe, New York, New York

The same technique works under education:

EDUCATION:
Technical Training, Workshops and Seminars (numerous)

Now look over your resume and see if anything is annoying to you. If it is, it is probably not true, or not you. If it is not true, take it out. If it is not you, but it is true and it will improve your candidacy, *try to leave it in.* This is no time to be humble.

The acid test for whether your resume is true is this: Would you be comfortable sharing this resume with your references? If so, go for it. If not, it is probably misleading or overstated in a way that will get you in trouble later anyway. Work it over until it is background check-proof.

I know from experience that some people are not comfortable with profiles that state their skills and abilities. If everything in your profile is true, factual, and not pompous, then go with it. If you are using your resume inside your own company, or applying to a position through a direct, guaranteed contact, then you might decide to drop your profile. (If you do drop your profile, save the wording.

Often it can be included in your cover letter, sometimes verbatim.) Without the profile, your resume will be better because you wrote a profile first, and it helped focus your thoughts throughout. If you are going to face heavy, direct competition—or if you are applying to people who are in no way obligated to speak with you—then I would recommend you use the best profile you can write.

Finally, check your resume for point of view one last time. Is everything really in the order of maximum desired impact on the reader? Take your time with this. The order of your information is second in importance only to the information itself. Think about your reader. **Put your information in order of interest to your targeted reader.**

Double check your consistency. Are titles treated the same throughout? Did you write "%" in one place and "percent" somewhere else? Did you spell out "six" in one place and write numerals, such as "4" or "2" in another? Is every word spelled right? Except for the grammar, spelling, and consistency, do not be a perfectionist. A perfectionist will still be working on her resume long after you have a great new job.

Final Design and Production

Typically, you want 12-, 11-, or, at smallest, 10-point font, with one-inch margins on the top, bottom, and sides. Use a common font, nothing too creative or weird. Don't be surprised if you have to tinker with your resume to get the design just right. Fonts and type sizes can be persnickety, and you sometimes have to take out a word to get a line or paragraph to fit the way you want.

Lean back and look at the resume on full-page view. Does it look crisp? Consistent? Attractive? Is this work that you would want to represent your company?

If the answer is yes, you're done.

You should email your resume in a universal format, which means Word (.doc or .docx) or Acrobat (.pdf). If you are worried about someone altering your resume, put it into a read-only format in Acrobat. To do this, you have to go one step up from the free Acrobat "reader" version. See www.acrobat.com or www.adobe.com/products/acrobat/ for more info. Corel also has a .pdf conversion and control feature; see http://www.corel.com/content/pdf/wpx4/edition-comparison-chart.pdf. If you don't already own these applications, however, they can get expensive fast. The easiest thing to do, especially if you need your resume *overnight,* is to just submit it in Word (from any Mac or PC platform).

If you are going to submit it to a company web site and they want you to copy and paste it into an edit box, be sure that all the features translate, so that "voilà" and "entrée" don't become "voila" and "entree," for example, and "don't" doesn't become "don*t" or "don&t" or worse.

Warning: People who do not know you will not open an unsolicited attachment. So in that case consider copying the entire resume *into the body of the email.* You can also attach it if you want. So you might say in your email, "My resume follows and is also attached in MS Word."

If you need a cover letter or email to go with your resume, turn to chapter 16 beginning on page 111.

If you're going to a meeting in person, you will need paper copies of your documents. Use standard-size white paper. If you use pink paper you'd better be applying for a job as a nail colorist. Otherwise, just stick to white. The weight of the paper matters, if you want something to obsess about. For management-level candidates, I recommend heavy paper, as it subconsciously denotes a candidate of substance, and feels different in the hand. If it has a watermark, make sure it prints right-side up. The paper is really not that big a deal, but you never know what can be a tipping factor.

Congratulations! Your overnight resume is done.

Scannable Resumes, e-Versions, Portfolios, and Reference to Websites or Social Networking Profiles

You are going to run into references to some special formats as you conduct a job search. You may see in postings or on job-search blogs references to scannable versions of a resume, or portfolio resumes. An employer may request an e-version of your documents. And some career coaching experts will recommend you use your own web site or a social networking profile as part of your search. Let's address those issues here.

Most employers are perfectly happy to receive your MS Word (.doc or .docx) or Adobe (.pdf) attachment, which they can dump directly into their computer databases for recruiting and staffing. A few old school companies still use scanners, but almost nobody uses them exclusively. If anyone asks you for a "scannable resume," all you have to do is:

1. Remove all typeface changes, that is, no bold, no italics, no underlining of any kind. ALL-CAPS remain acceptable.

2. Remove the border-to-border line you would normally put under your address, and any other lines, graphs, or drawings.

3. Remove all bullets, foreign notations, and symbols, so no •, ©, ®, ¥, £, ¶, è, and so on.

4. Make every single line start on the left margin, that is, the whole resume has the same left margin.

That's a scannable resume.

An e-version of your resume is simply an electronically transmissible version, most commonly, MS Word or Adobe. That's no big deal.

A portfolio resume is a resume that has hyperlinks in it linking to supporting material. So if you describe a project, say a marketing plan, the words "marketing plan" will be a hyperlink taking the reader to the actual plan. A mention of a patent may link to a copy of the actual patent. You can link to work products, pictures of you receiving awards, sound files of you giving a speech, ad infinitum, but it's probably a good idea to use this sparingly. Only artists should link to anything complex or confusing. Embedding links into resumes is a brilliant innovation in a business document that has only evolved slowly over the last few decades. You can take any resume and link words to supporting materials. Just don't overdo it.

Should you build a web site to support your job search? Sure, why not? Build a web site that shows your skillset and represents your accomplishments. For example, if you are a corporate trainer, you could build a web site showcasing the range of your abilities, perhaps providing a short video of you actually training a class, and demonstrating an actual CBT module you had designed. What you don't want to do is spend six months on this, because it's totally optional. Someone who spent the same effort on her job search would have a great new job while you're still trying to get your flash video to debug. Portfolio resumes are obviously never paper resumes; they live their whole lives as computer-based documents.

And referring people to your social networking profile is okay, but no big deal. If you have information that they need to know, it should be on your resume, not hidden on your LinkedIn profile. By the way, clean up your online presence. This is particularly important for young people, who seem to have missed the memo about professionalism and discretion. Recruiters routinely check your social networking pages, and your privacy settings are easier to breech than you might think. So no nude cocaine photos, no drunken revelry, no stories about anonymous sex, no escapades (photo or narrative) involving the police, or close calls with the police. Even cursing or strong political opinions are out. You can put all that back up after you have a solid new job (and pass your probationary period).

Additional Assistance

The following chapter contains complete samples of well-designed resumes. Look them over as a guide. You can copy styles, of course, but do not copy any sentences verbatim. Resume styles change and evolve, and today's hot phrase is tomorrow's cliché. (For instance, it's the opposite of progressive to use the word "progressive," "cutting edge" is passé, and "pioneering" is positively arcane.) The best way to make sure your resume is fresh is by writing it yourself.

If you decide you need additional help, there are two good sources: your friends, and a resume-writing professional.

Do not be worried or surprised if you get ten different opinions when you show your resume to six different friends. Use the principles outlined in this book and your own good judgment to sort through their suggestions for the ones you think are valid.

If you use a resume-writing professional, ask to see their samples, make sure the design is good, make sure they actually wrote the samples they are showing you, then actually read them. Your writer should have a good, honest approach. Hype and fluff are damaging to a well-qualified candidate.

You have every right to have assistance with your resume, by the way. The president of the United States, or United Airlines, or the United Way has help when he or she writes a speech. Unless you're applying to be a resume writer, and perhaps even then, you'd better get the best advice of friends, colleagues, and maybe a pro.

Finally, Please Don't *Oversell* Yourself

It is your job to sell yourself. Except in the worst of economic times, try to make every job change a promotion. (Of course, in the worst of economic times for your industry or area, a compromise may be in order. Any job may be a good job, then.) Readers of your resume will expect you to *truthfully* promote yourself.

Some of the advice in this book is pretty aggressive. My clients are generally fairly aggressive. They are committed to advancing their careers and to performing in the positions they take. They do not use aggressive techniques to get jobs they don't deserve and cannot manage; they use these techniques to get jobs they do deserve and can excel in.

If you inflate your background to apply for jobs for which you are not qualified, and for which you have not substantiated any material interest to date, and for which you are not prepared, then you will not succeed. Don't underestimate recruiters and hiring managers. Eventually you will be talking to a human being, and you will have to explain all the content of your resume.

If you are really interested in a career path, research it. Find people who are excelling in the field and ask them for their advice.

Do not abuse the techniques in this book. Use them to get the very best job in which you can excel. Nothing more, nothing less.

Take a look at your final draft. Is it the truth? It can be the prettiest version of the truth, yes, but it has to be the truth.

13 Sample Resumes

Phoebe McCoyne

12 Martinique Court, No. 2F
New York, New York 10014

pmcoyn283@gmail.com
Store Office: (212) 555-1398
Cell (24/7): (212) 555-9356

INTERESTS

Store Management • Sales Management • Customer & Private-Book Development
Highlights:
- One of the top 25 sales associates nationwide (out of several thousand).
- Trained in consultative and suggestive selling.
- Consistently proven ability to develop sales skills in subordinates.
- Proven manager and supervisor; advanced skill with business analysis and business writing.
- No restrictions on assignment or relocation for continued advancement.
- Fluent in French, proficient in Spanish.

Also: Proven affinity for high-end customer; expert at building private-book clientele; able to bond with customers and establish lasting relationships. Enduring contribution to the bottom line and quality of experience on behalf of every employer. Enthusiastic attitude.

EXPERIENCE

BEANSTALKS, HQ: Los Angeles, CA   2009–Present
Store Manager, Manhattan

Brought on board as opening manager for the new Manhattan store, a concept store designed to test merchandising ideas for the entire Beanstalks chain. Trained in Beverly Hills and San Francisco prior to opening in Manhattan. Supervise 20 stock and sales associates, providing sales training, operational expertise, and informal motivational coaching to all staff. Analyze sales, margins, trends. Coordinate with buyers in Los Angeles.
- Participated in final stages of store design. Represented Beanstalks to the contractor.
- Wrote merchandising and advertising plans for opening. Hired and trained opening staff.
- Exceeded original sales plan by 29 percent through sales training and coaching.

NORDSTROM, HQ: Seattle, WA   2007–2009
Section Sales Manager and **Sales Associate,** Beverly Hills, San Francisco

Top performer with the most successful major retailer in the nation. Selected to sales manage Brass Cherry, the top volume department at Nordstrom San Francisco Centre, one of the showcase stores in the chain. Sold, coached others in sales, analyzed sales, margins, and trends, reported to management. Trained to develop private-book business.
- One of the top 25 sales associates nationwide.
- Top sales performer on the floor with concurrent management duties.
- "Department All Star" and "Sales Pacesetter" awards.

AMERICAN CONGRESS ON FITNESS, HQ: Washington, DC   2005–2006
Outreach Representative (Sales)

Developed lines of communication with national and international accounts, selling educational items and licensed exercise apparel. Practiced suggestive selling. Prepared and processed all purchase orders, including international sales. Troubleshot orders, including "walking" them through the system when needed.
- Represented American Congress on Fitness at national convention in Chicago, 2006.

GOOD SHEPHERD HOSPITAL, HQ: Milwaukee, WI   Summer 2004
Intern, Public Relations

EDUCATION

B.A., **Speech Communications,** *summa cum laude,* Marquette University, Milwaukee, WI   2005

Darwin Ewoldt

1946 Chestnut Street
San Francisco, California 94109
(415) 555-7130
evolve@gamester.com

PASSION:
Design & Development of AAA Game Titles

GAME DEVELOPMENT:
- ➡ Experienced with Max, Maya, Renderware Studio, Perforce & Photoshop as well as proprietary tools.
- ➡ Technical artist and level/environment artist, including object and collision geometry creation, texture and material creation and mapping, special effects animation, particle effects, and some scripting.
- ➡ Experience with Wii, PSP, X-Box, Gamecube, PS2,Playstation, and Dreamcast. Also with multiplatform game development using cross-platform export systems for closely staggered release dates and unique localized/regionalized releases.
- ➡ Worked closely with engineers to develop and implement new gameplay features, data flow optimizations, rendering techniques, and proprietary animation tool development.
- ➡ In charge of exporting assets and fixing bugs on major portions of art assets during beta periods.

EMPLOYMENT:
LOCOMOTIVE GAMES (THQ), Santa Clara, California, 2006–Present
Game Designer
Contributing Artist:
- ➡ **Destroy all Humans: Big Willy Unleashed**: Particle effects and special effects, cutscene animations blocking, some scene scripting. Released for the Wii. Published by THQ.
- ➡ **Disney Pixar: Ratatouille**: Object modeling with animation and destructible states with Havok. Effects and particle systems. Released for PSP. Published by THQ, BuenaVista.
- ➡ **Disney Pixar: Cars**: Object modeling with animation and destructible states with Havok. Effects and particle systems. Released for PSP. Published by THQ, BuenaVista.
- ➡ **Power Rangers Dino Thunder**: Object modeling with animation and destructible states with Havok. Effects particle systems. Released on Playstation 2 and Gamecube. Published by THQ, BuenaVista.

Z-AXIS (bought by Activision), Foster City/Hayward, California, 2002–2005
Game Designer
Contributing Artist:
- ➡ **BMX XXX**: Particle effects, level and environment artist, and textures. Released on Playstation 2, X-Box, and Gamecube. Published by Acclaim.
- ➡ **Dave Mirra Freestyle BMX 2**: Level and environment artist, textures. Released on Playstation 2, X-Box, and Gamecube. Published by Acclaim.
  Greatest hits edition also released.
- ➡ **Dave Mirra Freestyle BMX Maximum Remix**: Level and environment artist, and textures. Released on Playstation. Published by Acclaim.
- ➡ **Dave Mirra Freestyle BMX**: Level and environment artist and textures. Released on Playstation and Dreamcast. Published by Acclaim.
  Double platinum title. Over 2 million copies sold.

ACCOLADE (bought by Infogames, then Atari), San Jose, California, 2001–2002
Game Designer
Contributing Artist:
- ➡ **McGrath vs. Pastrana Freestyle Motorcross:** Level and environment artist, and textures. Released on Playstation. Published by Acclaim.
- ➡ **Test Drive Offroad 3:** Texture artist (subcontract). Released on Playstation & Dreamcast. Published by Infogrames (Accolade).

Leander M. Hamilton II

23 Pinehurst Circle
Denver, Colorado 80235

lmh-hotsauce@global.com
Cell: (303) 555-2296

PROFILE

F & B Operations (multiunit or major operations, including resort and hospitality)

Background of proven success in entrepreneurial restaurant/F&B endeavors. Combination of M.B.A. financial and analytical skills, staffing and operations expertise, and marketing/promotions savvy. Experience features timely involvement with new concept formula restaurants, as well as grounding in highly controlled, corporate, and fast-food operations. Strengths include:

- Concept, image, and menu development
- Design of policies and procedures
- Training of management-level staff
- Training of operations-level staff
- Quality assurance (top-to-bottom, front-to-back)
- New product development
- Operational control (waste, loss, labor, inventory, cost, and cash control)

Other strengths include extensive experience with international kitchen and work crews and knowledge of international foods. "Kitchen proficiency" in French, Spanish, Tagalog.

EDUCATION

Golden Gate University, San Francisco, California
M.B.A., Management

Culinary Institute of America, Hyde Park, New York
Certificate, Professional Chef Training & Kitchen Management

California State University, Sonoma, California
B.A., English, and B.S., Political Science (double degree)

MANAGEMENT EXPERIENCE

The Palm, Barbados, West Indies   2009–2010
Consultant

Start-up consultant on this new restaurant. Contributed to all stages: concept and image development, restaurant design, construction supervision, equipment layout and installation, menu development.

- Hired and trained opening staff. Trained chef and asst. chef on recipes.
- Succeeded with extensive negotiations and lobbying with local government officials to win necessary regulatory approvals (and without resorting to graft).
- Completed business launch under projected timeline and on projected budget.
- Achieved positive cash flow for the owner and turned over the operation as scheduled. Excellent recommendation available.

continued

Charley's House (a PepsiCo franchise), Sacramento, California   2006–2009
General Manager

Charley's House is a casual family restaurant concept with a budget menu. The chain is well established in California and is scheduled to go national. Assigned the highest-volume restaurant in the Sacramento region.

- Achieved 24.5 percent cost of sales, bottom-line operating profit in excess of 32.25 percent.
- Managed first unit in region to break $1 million in sales.
- Raised quality assurance scores from the F to C range to a solid B.
- Facilitated R&D for new product roll out.
- Appointed to the Manager Review Board (regional).

Leander M. Hamilton Associates, San Francisco, California   2003–2004
Restaurant Consultant

- **Clark's**, London, England. Start-up consultant. Set up kitchen and menu. Trained initial chef and kitchen staff.
- **Polo Lounge**, Bangkok, Thailand. Marketing consultant. Developed marketing plan to attract more tourists and American clientele. Revised bar list.
- **The Carlisle Club**, Barbados, West Indies. Redesigned bar operations at popular nightclub.

Mill Restaurant, Coconut Grove, Florida   2002–2003
Manager

Hired to turn around negative sales trend in established restaurant with good name recognition but uneven operations.

- Increased profit margin from negative to 28 percent.
- Reestablished relations with better hotel and tour operators.

Le Parite Restaurant, Coconut Grove, Florida   2001–2002
Manager

- Achieved a ★★★ rating, one of the very few in the state.

COOKING EXPERIENCE

Guest Chef, Narsai's, Kensington, California
Sous Chef, Commercial Club, San Francisco, California
Line Cook, Scandia Restaurant, Los Angeles, California

ADDITIONAL

Additional experience in Europe, West Indies, Southeast Asia, Caribbean.

MENUS ON REQUEST

Ruth Ann Waters

raw@lawserv.ss.org
1351 Seminole Street, #6
Miami, Florida 33133
(305) 555-5946

SKILLS

Administrative Management/General Office/Secretarial
- Efficient, good-natured, good reputation with all former employers
- IBM and Mac expertise in all common office suites
- Basic accounting/bookkeeping
- Fast learner
- Accurate

EDUCATION

Miami/Dade Community College, Miami, Florida   degree expected 9/2011
Associate of Applied Arts (Concentration: Legal Office Management)

Hialeah High School, Miami, Florida   degree 6/2005
Diploma (College Preparatory Studies)

EXPERIENCE
(while student)

United States District Court, Miami, Florida   2010–Present
Administrative and File Clerk (official title: Clerk II)
- File memos, correspondence, and research to cases. Research cases from law books, Nexis, Lexis, and LawSearch; provide judicial clerks with printouts. Successfully perform all duties in an atmosphere where accuracy and the ability to follow detailed orders are critical. Cleared three-month filing backlog in three weeks.

Host Systems, Miami, Florida   2009
Office Assistant
- Maintained clean and well organized office at the headquarters of this corporate food service company. Also served as office courier.

Lechter's Housewares, Miami, Florida   2009
Assistant Manager (official title: Second Key)
- Managed store in absence of manager and assistant manager. Opened and closed out registers. Sold and supervised. Earned rapid promotion.

Cruise Time, Miami, Florida   2008–2009
Office Assistant
- Maintained cruise member account information. Answered incoming phones. Handled all errands as office courier. Some accounting projects as assigned.

Alcott & Andrews, Miami, Florida   2007
Stocker

ADDITIONAL KEYWORDS

Quickbooks, Quicken, payroll, P/R, A/R, A/P, billing, HTML, Web Page Design, receptionist, legal secretary, correspondence, B.A., Excel, MS Word, CaseTrak

Li (Henry) Wong

Hawkins Hall, Room 11315, 430 Wood Street, West Lafayette, IN 47906/wongli@purdue.edu/(765) 555-7650

SUMMARY OF QUALIFICATIONS

- **Global Supply Chain Management, Sourcing-Purchasing-Procurement, Vendor Management**
- Global manufacturing experience (logistics, project management, engineering, operations, liaison)
- Represent Chinese government-owned corporations to global partners (U.S., Canadian, E.U., African)
- Citizen of China, Permanent Resident of Canada; prefer English-speaking assignment in Canada or U.S.

EDUCATION

Master of Business Administration (MBA)   May 2010

Krannert School of Management, Purdue University, West Lafayette, IN

Honors & Activities:

> Operations Club, Consulting Club, Global Investment Group, Logistics Club, Chinese Business Association
> Krannert Academic Performance Scholarship; The World Bank Scholarship

Certifications:

> ISO9000 Internal Auditor Certificate

Bachelor of Electric and Electronic Engineering   June 2000

Wuhan University of Technology, Wuhan, China

Research:

> Elite Cup Thesis Competition, Energy Development and Usage in China (3rd prize)

EXPERIENCE

Star-Brite International Inc., Toronto, Canada   Summer 2009

A Canadian global logistics management company

> MBA Intern, B2B Sales

- Made out-bound cold calls to Chinese businesses and solicited RFPs for logistics consulting. Enrolled companies into Star-Brite's global business directory. Effectively helped company expand market share and market intelligence in Chinese business communities.
- Assisted senior managers in refining their strategic business development plans re China.

Pinggao Group, Pingdingshan, Henan, China

China's leading manufacturer and distributor of high- and ultra high-voltage switchgear equipment, listed in A share stock market with a registered capital of US$400 Million and annual turnover of US$250 Million

> Overseas Project Manager   2005–2007

- Assembled a crossfunctional team to address business negotiations, product designs, operation processes, and distribution issues for each new project. Created project schedule and milestones, directed global and Chinese purchasing, established inspection/testing/diagnostics, and wrote installation procedures as required.
- Initiated over 10 country market research studies by employing statistical models; analyzed competitive market intelligence, and designed and evaluated marketing strategies.
- Collaborated with Chinese government-owned corporations such as CMEC (China National Machinery and Equipment Import & Export Corporation) on bidding and implementation of important international electric projects, including Merowe Project, China's largest export project of electricity power transmission and distribution line.
- Successfully expanded European market and awarded Spain GIS project, the first European deal for Pinggao Group.
- Participated in overseas promotion programs, such as trade shows and client site visits; developed strong relationships with business partners.

> Product Engineer   2003–2005

- Designed products in accordance with customer specifications and requirements.

> Production Assistant   2000–2002

- Effectively managed, motivated, and trained workforce of 15 production crew members for three shifts.

SPORT

Chinese rules Table Tennis (nationally ranked)

Michele T. Tiger

1323 Maui Drive, Apt. D-218 · Baton Rouge, Louisiana 70803
(225) 555-3202 • mtiger5@lsu.edu

EMPHASIS

Environmental Engineering

EDUCATION

Louisiana State University (LSU), Baton Rouge, Louisiana

Bachelor of Science in Environmental Engineering, May 2010, GPA in Engineering: 4.0

Minor: Business Administration

> *Related Coursework:* Qualitative Water Management, Control and Treatment of Urban Runoff, Hazardous Waste Management, Lakes & Watersheds Management and Modeling, Spectrometry & Microscopy (Advanced Bench Lab), Sampling Techniques (Advanced Field Lab)

EXPERIENCE

Guehler Bros. Environmental Consultants, New Orleans, Louisiana

Intern (Field Engineer), August 2010–Present

- Under supervision of senior engineer, assist with home inspections (mold and toxin)
- Use both destructive and nondestructive sampling techniques
- Sample inside air and compare it to exterior air samples
- Assess possible contamination sources in home purchases
- Prepare remediation plans for mold and toxin contaminations

Dow Chemicals, Houston, Texas

Engineering Co-Op (Infrastructure Engineering), Spring 2009

- Analyzed survey reports, maps, drawings, and blueprints to plan new plants and improvements
- Estimated quantities and cost of material, equipment, and labor using formulae
- Tested soils to determine foundation requirements for concrete and steel structures
- Tested brownfield sites to identify pre-construction soil remediation requirements

Louisiana State University, Baton Rouge, Louisiana

Tutor, Summers and Falls, 2007, 2008, 2009

- Beginning chemistry and physics

OTHER

Sales Associate, TigerMania, Baton Rouge, Louisiana, December 2009–Present

Barista, Our House Coffee House, Baton Rouge, Louisiana, Spring 2008

COMPUTER SKILLS

AutoCAD, MS Word, Excel, PowerPoint, Intergraph, RISA, FloatingPoint Scheduler, VersionControl

HONORS

Tuition Opportunity Program for Students (TOPS) Scholarship, National Society of Collegiate Scholars, Alpha Lambda Delta Honor Society

ACTIVITIES

American Society of Civil Engineers, Lambda Lambda Lambda Fraternity, Habit for Humanity, Tiger Athletic Foundation

Aiden S. Hargrove

hargon@alumni.bostoncollege.edu
cell: (650) 555-9234

West Coast address:
1749 Post Street
Belmont, California 94002

East Coast address:
5 Colliston Road, Apt. 7
Brighton, Massachusetts 02135

KNOWLEDGE

Biochemical Manufacturing/Protein Purification

Small- and large-scale Amicon chromatography columns. Romicon and Millipore ultrafiltration cartridges. Continuous feed Alfa Laval centrifuges. Gaulins homogenizers. Various centrifugal and displacement pumps. Waters Millipore HPLC. Small-scale lyophilizing equipment. Hewlett-Packard spectrophotometers. Large-scale, in-place stainless steel tanks. Large- and small-scale glycol heat exchangers. Amsco glassware washers and driers. Finn Aqua and Amsco autoclaves. MS Office Suite (Word, Excel, PowerPoint).

EXPERIENCE

Genentech, Inc., South San Francisco, California
Product Recovery Operations
Senior Technician, 2009–2010

Conducted large- and small-scale recovery and purification of proteins utilizing ultrafiltration and chromatography processes in a GMP environment. Coordinated day-to-day purification activities for marketed products. Oriented new staff. Wrote and revised GMP tickets and SOPs for specific manufacturing processes, e.g., wrote the SOPs for steam sterilizing of in-place and portable stainless steel tanks and associated filters used in the final purification facility.

Also provided technical support on purification processes to R&D labs working with HPLC and lyophilizing equipment. Assisted in scaling up projects from R&D into clinical trials, including revision of GMP documents and SOPs to facilitate transition.

Lab Services Technician, 2008

Acid washing of organic chemistry glassware used in production and R&D. Maintained sufficient supplies of sterile lab equipment to meet production and R&D requirements.

Boston College, Biology Department, Chestnut Hill, Massachusetts
Research Assistant, 2007–2008

Research assistant for D. Y. C. Ting in his cytogenetics laboratory, experimenting with Maize tissue. Prepared culture media and maintained records of experimental media compositions. Analyzed tissue culture response. Directed pilot experiment with Teosinte tissue culture. Ordered supplies and equipment.

ADDITIONAL SKILLS

Genetics: Electrophoretic determination of DNA molecules. Preparation and observations of mammalian chromosomes. Identification of regions of DNA using Southern Blotting. Study of inheritance patterns of mutant traits in Drosophila.

Chemistry: Qualitative and quantitative analysis, pH titrations, spectrophotometry, column and thin-layer chromatography, chemical extractions, recrystallization, distillation.

EDUCATION

Boston College, Chestnut Hill, Massachusetts
B.S., Biology, and **B.A., Philosophy** (double degree), 2007

DEAN RODGERS

safety@olseninc.com

Olsen Equipment Co., Inc.
874 Gerard Street
Mandeville, LA 70448
154 Cayman Cove
Mandeville, LA 70448

Office Direct Line: (504) 555-9616
Office General Line: (504) 555-9931
Mobile (voice/text): (504) 555-3534
Fax: (504) 555-4074
Residence/Message: (504) 555-9142

PROFILE

Over 30 years in trucking and transportation

Expertise
- Safety, Safety Programs, Driver Training
- Logistics
- Special Permit Loads

Honors
- Over 3,000,000 miles without an accident
- Outstanding series of awards and honors for safe driving from employers and The American Trucking Association

EXPERIENCE

OLSEN EQUIPMENT CO., INC. — Mandeville, LA
Training Supervisor/Safety Officer — 2009–Present

Olsen moves oil exploration and roadbuilding heavy equipment and permitted loads throughout Louisiana, Texas, Arkansas, and Mississippi.

Hire, train, and coordinate drivers, owner/operators, and escort contractors. Perform background investigations on drivers. Manage licensing records on drivers to insure proper credentials and status. Administer random drug-testing program in compliance with state and federal laws. Represent company to state and federal regulatory authorities and insurance carriers. Maintain company safety programs and create new safety programs as needed. Maintain knowledge of state and interstate regulations impacting operations. Foster an environment of care and consideration for the rules of the road and for the communities in which we operate.

Delegate daily assignments for owned and leased trucks. Maintain all work records for trucks and drivers. Prepare payroll, trip, and lease payments for payroll department. Ensure driver discipline and compliance with company policies and regulations. Select and train company representatives to be our eyes and ears out on the road.

CONTINENTAL BAKING CO. — Tulsa, OK
Transport Driver — 2000–2008

Drove approximately 600,000 accident-free miles in Oklahoma, Kansas, Arkansas, Missouri, and other states. Member, Safety Committee (appointed by union). Oriented and field tested new drivers. Numerous honors and awards.

SAFEWAY STORES — Tulsa, OK
Transport Driver — 1996–2000

Drove four years accident free in Texas, Oklahoma, Arkansas, Missouri and other states.

CHIEF FREIGHT LINES — Tulsa, OK
Transport Driver

Drove all combinations of tractor-trailer rigs over-the-road throughout Midwest, Atlantic Seaboard, Northeast, approximately 2,500,000 miles, all accident free, and including haz mat loads.

Caleb Coleman Davis

ccd@alumni.UCSB.edu

2114 San Tomas Court
Santa Barbara, California 93105

Cell (24 hr. voice/txt):
(805) 555-1280

INTEREST   **Failure Engineering**

EDUCATION   **California State Polytechnic University (Cal Poly)**   San Luis Obispo, California
                B.S., Mechanical & Civil Engineering   2010

Self-designed Concentration: Safety Engineering & Failure Analysis
Thesis: *Analysis of a Walkway Failure: Eight Stages of Error*

Pertinent Coursework:

- Human Factors
- Materials Science
- Infrastructure Design
- Roads & Traffic
- Design Lab
- History of Science
- Electromechanics
- Advanced Statistics
- Research Methodology
- Industrial Hygiene
- Site Safety
- Information Science

Special Skill: 3-D Modeling on Computer
Honors: Graduated magna cum laude, Dean's Honors, 2007–2010, GPA: 3.84

EXPERIENCE **Baker, White, Dean, DeOme Engineering**   Oakland, California
                Failure Engineer (Co-Op)   Jan–Aug 2009

- Junior member of a team that investigated structural, chemical, biological, biochemical, and electrical accidents in industrial, research, medical, and public facilities throughout the United States and Canada.

- Multidisciplinary team included engineers, scientists, industrial psychologists, and other specialists as needed.

- Performed experiments and calculations to determine source(s)/cause(s) of accidents. Prepared case reports detailing system/procedural flaws.

- Special project: Researched handling, storage, transportation, and disposal of infectious materials leaving hospitals, including regulatory requirements.

Underwriters Laboratory   San Jose, California
Laboratory Technician (Intern)   Summer 2008

- Hands-on experience testing consumer electrical products including voltage surge protectors, hair driers, RC toy cars, inverters, lighting ballasts, and similar.

- Gained experience with oscilloscopes, multimeters, logic analyzers, frequency counters, signal generators, and other bench tools.

- Disassembled products, conducted testing, recorded data, wrote summaries of findings.

- Participated in "Murphy's Law" sessions with senior engineers, creative brainstorming sessions to imagine potential consumer misuse of products.

Davis Electric   Santa Barbara, CA
Electrician's Helper   Summers, 2004–2007

SPORTS   **Captain, Cal Poly Sailing Team**

- Planned and coordinated weekly regattas involving up to 40 competing students and a top-heavy official race committee of 10.

- Obtained club sponsorship by the San Luis Obispo Yacht Club, including underwriting competitive events and purchase of two new boats.

PI QI LING

pling@ucon.edu

STRENGTHS

Human Resources-Generalist/Consultant/Special Projects Manager

Senior human resources generalist with strong international orientation and experience in recruiting, staffing, compensation, communications, HRIS, benefits, ERISA, organization development and internal consulting, and ROI/cost benefit/P&L analysis. Successful HR management experience in U.S. and abroad. Have originated, developed, and managed key HR functions for new business unis. Key participant in strategic decision-making. Multidisciplinary experience: human resources, operations, financials. Native fluency in English and Mandarin Chinese; conversationally fluent in French, Japanese, and several Chinese dialects.

EDUCATION

M.B.A., The Wharton School, University of Pennsylvania, Philadelphia, Pennsylvania
B.A., Mathematics-Economics (double major), Reed College, Portland, Oregon

EXPERIENCE

WHALEN-MASTERS INTERNATIONAL, Stamford, Connecticut
International Human Resources Consultant, 2009–Present

Engaged by director of international human resources to provide full-scope generalist support to 10 international joint ventures in start-up to fully-operational status, $48 million total seed monies, 32 interlocked business partners, initial staffing targets of 600+.

Select contributions:

- Improved customer service to clients by developing "single point of contact" structure.
- Established recruiting and staffing processes, identified new sources for technical contractors, and designed and implemented new tracking and reporting methods.
- Redesigned international programs by benchmarking best practices, evaluating vendors, and identifying productivity enhancements.
- Structured short- and long-term employment packages for international assignees.

MORROW TECHNOLABS, INC., Boston, Massachusetts
Human Resources Consultant, Taiwan, 2008

As the only human resources expert on a technical team of 36, designed and installed a DB2 Human Resources System for a national company with 12 regional offices and 40,000 employee records.

Select contributions:

- Developed business statement and detailed conversion plan; assisted client in designing all HR programming.
- Extensive formal and informal knowledge transfer/training to client and United Nations consultants involved with this project.

MIEJING USA, Los Angeles, California (formerly The Harmony Companies, see below)
VP & Merger Team Member, Human Resources, M-USA HQ, 2007

Consulted closely with country managers to resolve issues related to merger of Asian operations with a U.S.-based acquisition, The Harmony Companies, comprised of 24 U.S. and offshore facilities and 4300 affected staff in 12 countries. This was a fast-paced project, with heavy load of daily communications as project parameters, specifications, and objectives evolved.

Select contributions:

- Created process framework for post-merger staff selection and successfully represented the process to country managers. Managed process; provided counsel regarding contracts and staffing issues.
- Project managed the integration of key human resource-related activities by country to ensure resolution of critical issues by merger date.
- Developed reporting method for senior management to determine country-specific human resource support, staffing, and expense levels pre- and post-merger.
- Highest-ranking officer of The Harmony Companies offered a permanent position after reorganization.

continued

THE HARMONY COMPANIES, Los Angeles, California
VP of Human Resources, 2003–2006
Administered centralized human resources function for 4300 employees, 600 retirees, and 150 inactives, including international assignees. Managed staff of 16, planned and administered $2.8 million annual HR budget (aggregate), controlled $950,000 in U.S.-based assets.

Select contributions:
- Developed and successfully implemented statistical control practices which proved value added to top management; built credibility for human resources by linking HR strategies to business strategies and financial metrics.
- Managed proposed and actualized M&A integration involving businesses from 100 to 2000 employees.
- Project managed the introduction of flexible benefits corporate-wide in 10 months and within budget.
- Managed four departments, decreased staff by 23 percent, decreased total operating expenses by 17 percent.
- Served on Human Resources Information System (HRIS) Steering Committee.

CHEMEX BANK NT & SA, New York, New York
VP & Manager, Training, Asia Division, Human Resources, Regional HQ: Tokyo, Japan, Training HQ: Singapore, 1999–2003
Provided strategic direction and interpreted policy in human resources development relative to country-specific business plans, budgets and organizational development issues. In Singapore, supervised a core staff of 10 with diverse responsibility for instructional design, training, IS, and administration. Functionally responsible for developing and training personnel officers in all 15 division countries.

Select contributions:
- Created new revenue stream of more than $1 million over four-year period by designing, negotiating contracts, and delivering fee-based training services to Korean correspondent banks, financial institutions, and government entities through our Singapore Center. First HR executive in history of the company to create a profit center of this size.
- Migrated corporate programs to 15 countries in the division as part of fundamental change in culture/strategy.
- Implemented corporate-wide performance planning, coaching, and evaluation process in Asia Division as part of move to standardize world practices.
- Engineered downsizing of eight full-time employees and trained local continuation successor, upon completion of change project.
- Managed design, development, and piloting of standardized global Credit Training Program.

Management Development Instructor, Corporate Human Resources

AVP & Head of Credit, Consumer Credit Card Center

Training Officer, Chemex New York

CONTINUING EDUCATION/PROFESSIONAL AFFILIATIONS
American Compensation Association Certification, in progress
Senior Professional in Human Resources (SPHR), Human Resource Certification Institute
Society for Human Resource Management
Institute for International Human Resources
Human Performance Technology Associates
American Society for Training & Development

AWARDS
Executive Incentive Plan Award, Restricted Stock Awards, Exceptional Performance Awards

14 Special Styles, More Solutions

Special Styles Matter

Some industries have evolved their own distinctive resume styles. If your resume is not in the appropriate style for your industry, then you will look like an outsider *even if you have the right experience*. For instance, believe it or not, airplane pilots and ship captains have their own style of resume. In this chapter, we will investigate a few of the more common style variations.

In some cases, the industry has a particular way of handling the information, and sometimes it just has a particular look that may be hard to describe but easy to show. Immediately following the narrative of this chapter are full-size samples of resumes that illustrate the points mentioned below. You may want to refer back and forth between the narrative and the samples to really get a feel for the different styles.

Curriculum Vitae or CV (medical, scientific, academic)

Samples: Joshua D. F. Gordon, Charyn Watkins, Larantomonga "Lara" Quantarangon

A curriculum vitae, or CV, as it is commonly known, is a highly stylized type of resume. This style is common in education, science, and medical fields, especially for credentialed professionals. College professors, scientists, and doctors (and students who want to become scientists, professors, or doctors) use CVs.

In CVs, education always comes first, even if you're 80 years old. An objective is not used, but a section headed "RESEARCH INTERESTS" or similar may take its place. You never brag in a CV, but academic honors may be retained decades after they have been earned. Paid employment is not particularly emphasized in a CV, and publications, presentations, research, and even classroom experiences may be featured. There is no length limit to a CV, and accomplished academics late in life may have CVs that are *dozens of pages long.* An important note for students is that "EXPERI-ENCE" may include full-time, part-time, paid, unpaid, and even volunteer experiences *mixed in together.* Bare listings, instead of narrative descriptions, are common. In a CV, job descriptions can be extremely brief or nonexistent.

For example, whereas in a regular job resume you might say "Developed curriculum for 'Intro-duction to Physics'; taught classes to three sections, a total of 180 students per semester; conceived of and assembled experimental demonstrations as a pedagogical technique; graded labs and papers; fielded student concerns in class and out," in a CV you would simply list:

Wolcott University, Centreville, Pennsylvania, 2009–2010
Instructor, "Introduction to Physics"

The careful choosing of headings organizes the experience in a CV. Thus, an experience such as being named a McNair Research Scholar could be listed under "EDUCATION" as an honor, or explicated more fully under "RESEARCH EXPERIENCES." Publications can be listed all together, or subdivided into "BOOKS," "ARTICLES," "CONFERENCE PROCEEDINGS," "ABSTRACTS," "BOOK REVIEWS," and "UNPUBLISHED PAPERS." The person designing the CV has to decide which design will have the most Wow Factor with the intended reader. Here are some common headings for CVs:

Research Interests	Education	Honors & Awards
Sample Research Projects	Research Experience	Lectures & Presentations
Publications	Teaching & Tutoring	Service & Leadership
Academic Conferences	Symposia	Practica
Committee Appointments	Patents	Licensure
Major Papers	Thesis	Dissertation
Laboratory Skills	Languages	Study Abroad
Student Activities	Scholarships & Fellowships	Assistantships
Grants	Exhibitions & Table Topics	Affiliations
Consulting	Translations	Additional

There are many variations of CVs. Dr. Gordon's CV is a classic model (see page 77). Note the human interest listing at the bottom, to distinguish this CV from what may be hundreds of others. The Charyn Watkins example illustrates how a student can feature classroom, internship, and field experiences over paid employment (see page 79). Paid employment, for students, is often irrelevant to their immediate goals. Finally, administrators may have CVs that have some of the features of resumes, such as more explication of duties and accomplishments. See Lara Quantarangon's example for that style on page 80.

For more examples of academic, medical, and scientific curricula vitae, find a copy of my classic monograph, *Asher's Bible of Executive Resumes*, or check out the CV sections of *From College to Career.*

Legal

Samples: Andrew Baxter Clay, Barbara J. Damlos

Attorneys' resumes are distinctive, but legal secretaries, paralegals, legal office administrators, and others in the legal field use standard resumes and should follow the resume instructions elsewhere in the book.

If you are an attorney, you should never put an objective on your resume; you are your objective. A border-to-border line under the address, universal in other resumes and CVs, is rare. Profiles are also rare, but if you have a specialty you can list it with a heading like one of these three examples:

EXPERTISE   Corporate Taxation
EMPHASIS   Employment Law
INTEREST   Environmental Law

Always write "v." instead of "vs." List "Member, State Bar of California," not "Member of the Bar, State of California" as bar membership is technically extragovernmental. Understatement is definitely the preferred tone, brevity the rule. It's also a good idea to put something interesting somewhere on these resumes to keep them from looking like ten thousand others. Note the nonlegal job on Andrew Baxter Clay's resume (page 82). Include journal publications and published opinions if available, as shown on the Barbara J. Damlos resume (page 83).

Finance

Samples: Marybeth Whitney-Winegrove, E. Edleff Schwaab

Finance resumes look a lot like attorneys' resumes, especially on the East Coast. This style may or may not have a profile, and small type and expansive white space contribute to the distinctive look. Most jobs in this sector are gotten by personal introduction and word of mouth, so resumes are noticeably less flashy than in other industries. On the West Coast , finance resumes tend to look more like regular business resumes. Most commercial bankers, insurance executives, and others in fields related to finance should design their resumes with a standard profile and appearance. See Whitney-Winegrove's example on page 84, and Schwaab on page 85.

Acting and Modeling

Sample: Andrea Tipton

Acting resumes are simply tables of performances. They are designed to fit onto the back of an eight-by-ten photograph, usually a head shot. The younger and less experienced the actor, the more training, church plays, and nebulous listings will be featured. As their careers progress, actors list only their best and most recent work, but always on an eight-by-ten sheet of paper. Acting resumes never list an actor's address. It will show the phone number only, or the phone number and address of the actor's agency. Modeling resumes are almost identical, just listing shoots, products featured, known photographers, and usually the name of the ad agency thrown in for good measure. Height and weight are standard listings, but race is never discussed. See page 86.

Art, Music, TV, and Film

Sample: Bruce Nolin

Studio musicians, TV and film people, cartoonists, and those with similar talents often have careers that consist of an unending series of projects, or "credits." Bruce Nolin's is an example of a credits-based resume, which is a good solution for this type of background. See page 87.

Artist's Bio

Sample: Marta Paulos

An artist's bio is a short biographical statement about her life and philosophy of art. This type of bio is particularly useful as it can be displayed in a gallery along with the artist's work. When applying to galleries, a bio like this would be paired with a credits-style resume showing training and a list of prior shows and awards. No address or phone is on the bio when it is hung at a show, as all contacts should be made through the gallery. See page 88.

Consultant's or Speaker's Vita

Sample: Nathaniel A. Robertson

Similar to an artist's biography, consultants' and speakers' vitae are third-person promotional pieces. These vitae are designed to be used in marketing a firm, justifying a firm's high fees, and introducing the principals at speaking engagements. Most speakers' bureaus write vitae like this on every speaker they represent. See page 89. Note that this style is most clearly not to be used for getting a job. Note that the singular of "vitae" is "vita." For more examples of vitae for speakers, consultants, and entire firms, see my book, *Asher's Bible of Executive Resumes.*

"Shuffle the Deck of Cards" Resume

Sample: Chrystal Ann Horton

Ms. Horton's background was spotty, with lots of jobs in lots of different industries, so the challenge was to create focus. Note how the repeated use of the subheading "duties" allows all the work histories to be written in the present tense? With the dates omitted, every single one of these jobs is interchangeable. They can be arranged and rearranged endlessly! We dropped and re-sorted jobs completely out of order to create this presentation and many others, all with the same source data. I would not recommend this for most candidates, but this client reported that she got tons of interviews and multiple offers with this resume. Simply amazing. See page 90.

Recent College Grad—No Work History

Sample: Dani S. Chesney

This candidate has never worked for pay one day in her life, yet following the guidelines in this book, she has put together a compelling first resume. If I did not point out the candidate's complete lack of paid work experience, you probably would not notice anything unusual about this resume at all. See page 91. Compare this example with the ones on pages 64 and 66, which highlight student employment.

Housecat

Sample: Ernie

This resume was written by my associate Susan Hall. Ernie was an actual cat she knew (although she does admit his accomplishments were inflated). See page 92.

Elementary School-Age Child

Sample: Calida L. Coleman

Calida L. Coleman's resume was written by her mother, and sent to me as a humorous example of how resume principles from this book can be applied to any background and any objective. See page 93.

JOSHUA D. F. GORDON, M.D.   **Curriculum Vitae**

820 Mill View Lane   jdfgmd@gmail.com
Los Altos Hills, California 94022   Telephone/voice/pager (24/7): (415) 555-0132

SPECIALTY   ANESTHESIOLOGY

CREDENTIALS

Board Eligible, American Board of Anesthesiology	2010
Basic Life Support Instructor	2010
Advanced Cardiac Life Support	2010
Diplomate, National Board of Medical Examiners	2007
Federal Licensure Examination	2006
Medical License, State of California	2005
Medical License, State of Ohio	2004

EXPERIENCE

Staff Anesthesiologist

Santa Clara Valley Medical Center, San Jose, California	2010–2011
Pacific Presbyterian Medical Center, San Francisco, California	2010–2011
Sonoma Valley Hospital, Sonoma, California	2011
Seton Medical Center, Daly City, California	2011

TRAINING

Research Fellowship (blood bank and liver transplant anesthesia)   2010
University of California, San Francisco

Residency (anesthesiology)   2007–2010
University of California, San Francisco

Internship (internal medicine)   2006–2007
University of California, San Francisco

EDUCATION

M.D., College of Medicine   2006
University of Cincinnati, Cincinnati, Ohio

A.B., Biochemical Sciences   2002
Princeton University, Princeton, New Jersey
    Thesis: *Studies on a Deletion Mutant from a Recombination Bacteriophage Library*

Three Advanced Levels (physics, chemistry, biology)	1998
Twelve Ordinary Levels	1996
Harrow School, Harrow-on-Hill, England	

continued

Joshua D. F. Gordon, M.D. C.V./page 2

RESEARCH

ARTICLES:

"A comparison of HTLV-1 Seropositivity in Orthotopic Liver Transplant Recipients Before and After Routine HTLV-1 Screening." J. D. F. Gordon, M.D.; E. Donegan, M.D. (in preparation).

"The Effect of Aprotinin on Intracranial Pressure and Cerebral Edema in Rabbits with Galactosamine-Induced Acute Liver Failure." J.D. F. Gordon, M.D.; M. C. Prager, M.D.; S. F. Ciricillo, M.D.; M. Grady, B.A. (submitted).

"Vecuronium Plasma Concentrations During Orthotopic Liver Transplantation in Humans." J. D. F. Gordon, M.D.; J. E. Caldwell, M.B.Ch.B.; M. C. Prager, M.D.; M. L. Sharma, Ph.D.; L. D. Gruenke, Ph.D.; D. M. Fisher, M.D.; N. Ascher, M.D., Ph.D.; R. D. Miller, M.D. (submitted).

"The Pharmacokinetics of Vecuronium During Liver Transplantation in Humans." J. D. F. Gordon, M.D.; J. E. Caldwell, F.F.A.R.C.S.; M. C. Prager, M.D.; M. L. Sharma, Ph.D.; L. D. Gruenke, Ph.D.; R. D. Miller, M.D. Anesth. Analg. 2010; 70: S432 (abstract, presented at the IARS 74th Congress, Honolulu, Hawaii, March 13, 2010).

ADDITIONAL:

"Fibrinolysis During Liver Transplantation," in association with Dr. Marie Prager, Department of Anesthesia, Dr. Marc Shuman and Dr. Larry Corash, Department of Hematology, UCSF, 2010.

"Analysis of Lymphocyte Subset Variations Associated with Liver Transplantation," in association with Dr. Elizabeth Donegan, Director of Blood Bank, UCSF, 2000.

AFFILIATIONS

American Society of Anesthesiologists	2008–Current
International Anesthesia Research Society	2008–Current
California Society of Anesthesiologists	2008–Current
Northern California Anesthesia Society	2008–Current

COMMUNITY SERVICE

Volunteer, Animal-Assisted Therapy Program, San Francisco SPCA	2009–Current
Instructor, Basic Life Support, American Red Cross, Southwest Ohio Chapter	2005–2006

PERSONAL INTERESTS

Interested in therapeutic aspects of animal-human relationships, especially as related to illness recovery and geriatrics. Hobbies include Weimaraner dogs and violin. Certified Grade VII (final) "with distinction" in violin, Board of Royal College of Music, London.

Charyn Watkins

cwat@alumni.michigan.edu
121 Valentine Circle
Lansdale, PA 19446
(215) 555-0827

INTERESTS

Nutrition and Animal Husbandry
- Rodent, canine, feline, equine, and primate nutrition, including pathologies.
- Laboratory techniques for microbiology, organic and biochemistry.
- Read, write, speak, translate German.

EDUCATION

University of Michigan, Ann Arbor, Michigan
B.S., Zoology, *summa cum laude,* 2010

Emphases

Microbiology - Parasitology - Metabolism - Evolution - Mammalian GI Tract

Lab Skills

Recombinant DNA technology, protein synthesis and regulation, plasmids and cloning, restriction endonucleases, organic chemistry, spectrophotometer, autoclave, chromatography titration, dissection, nutrient plate preparation, analysis of blood/urine/fecal/tissue samples.

RESEARCH

Prof. R. Heihnricht, University of Michigan, Summer 2009
Research assistant on field study in Kenya to investigate ecosystem coefficients to an outbreak of equine fever among Grevy's zebra, *Equus grevyi.* Site laboratory equipment manager (specimen collection and preparation). Sponsored in part by the Government of Kenya and NSF Grant 2009061/b.

Prof. W. Derr, University of Michigan, Spring 2009
Laboratory assistant in insect-insect parasitology research that served as the foundation for Prof. Derr's paper, "A micro-model of co-evolution," Jour.Bio.Sci. Dec., 2009, which won the NSF Lamarck Award for best paper on evolution.

Prof. Y. Yang, University of Michigan, Fall 2008
Conducted a literature survey to catalog abstracts and articles on all known water-producing fauna for a period of the last twenty years.

MAJOR PAPERS

"A Surprising Analysis of the Nutritional Properties of Major Brands of Rat Block: The Sum of the Parts ≠ Effect of the Whole," presented to the Regional Meeting of Research Animal Husbandry Professionals, Madison, Wisconsin, 2009.

"Toward a New Taxonomy: Some Logical Challenges as a Result of Recent Advances in Genetic Engineering," selected by the Michigan Undergraduate Science Journal as best undergraduate paper of 2008–2009 (Summer 2009, pp. 128–136).

"Metabolism and Exercise, or Why Laboratory Nutrition Data Don't 'Work Out,'" honors thesis presented to the Zoology Department, U. Mich., May 15, 2010.

EMPLOYMENT

University of Michigan, Ann Arbor, Michigan, 2009–2010
Teaching Assistant/Laboratory Assistant, Department of Zoology
- Prepared undergraduate laboratory teaching assignments for Prof. Yang.

University of Michigan, Ann Arbor, Michigan, 2006–2010
Husbandry Caretaker
- Cared for rats, mice, cats, and monkeys for the Depts. of Psychology, Biology, and Zoology. Relief caretaker in School of Agriculture and School of Veterinary Medicine, including working with raptors and ungulates.
- Initiated "Rats on Loan" program with local school district.

LARANTOMONGA "LARA" QUANTARANGON
Curriculum Vitae
Cell: 408-555-1985/laraq@sjsu.edu

Campus Address:
1244 Elm Street
San Jose, California 95112

Texas Address:
29241 Lone Star Hwy
Barnab, Texas 79205

Areas of Interest: **Residence Life (graduate & undergraduate)**
Student Activities & Special Events
Leadership Development
Greek Life

Education:

Texas Tech University, Lubbock, Texas
M.Ed., Higher Education Administration, May 2010

> Coursework included: Residence Life Management, College Personnel Administration, Legal Issues in the College & University Setting, Counseling, External Affairs, Public Administration & Management, Evaluation & Metrics, Issues in Race, Gender & Sexuality, Budgeting.

Baylor University, Waco, Texas
B.A., Women's Studies, minor in Marketing (Business), *cum laude*, May 2005

College & University Residence Life Experience:

Texas Tech M.Ed. Program, Lubbock, Texas
Field Study, Spring 2009

> Conducted a best-practices review of residence life programming at large public universities in Texas and California. Produced a 25-page research paper: "Best Practices in Residence Life Policies and Programming at Large Public Universities in Texas and California: There Is More than One Right Answer!"

San Jose State University, San Jose, California
Assistant Residence Life Director, 2007–2009

> Participated in every aspect of daily operations management for thirteen residence halls, 2200 rooms/suites, over 50 common areas including full kitchens, in-residence hall gyms, the commuter students' lounge, and a computer lab. On call 24/7 in absence of the Director. Hall Director for the graduate students' residence hall. Provided some input to capital and operating budgets. Assisted with staffing decisions (hiring/firing/development/discipline), total staff of 182.

Baylor University, Waco, Texas
Residence Hall Advisor, 2002–2005

> RHA for three different residence halls. In charge of health and welfare for mixed-gender freshmen residence halls (two years), and a drug-alcohol-and-tobacco-free floor for the final year.

Laratomonga "Lara" Quantarangon   CV/Page 2

Other College Employment:

> **Baylor University**, Waco, Texas
> **Tutor**, 2001–2005
>
> > Official tutor for the English department, peer tutor in the Writing Center.
>
> **Baylor University**, Waco, Texas
> **"Cage" Clerk**, 2001–2002
>
> > Counter person in the gym, checking IDs and checking out gym equipment.

Additional Leadership Experiences:

> **Sigma Epsilon Chi**, Baylor University, Waco, Texas
> **Treasurer, Pledge Week Spirit Coordinator, and Service Chair**, 2002–2005

Papers, Publications & Presentations:

Student Activities:

> —"Best Practices in Residence Life Policies and Programming at Large Public Universities in Texas and California: There Is More than One Right Answer!," presented during the M.Ed. residential intensive, Lubbock, Texas, June 22–25, 2009.
>
> —"Gen Y and U: What You Need to Know about Incoming Students," presented as a Res Life staff orientation talk, August 15, 2008.
>
> —"Why Students Choose a Drug-Alcohol-and-Tobacco-Free Residence Hall Option: Five Common Rationales, Most Having Nothing at All to Do with Drugs, Alcohol, or Tobacco," presented to Sociology 401, April 5, 2005.
>
> —"Why I Choose to Vote, Every Single Time," Letter to the Editor, *The Baylorean*, December 1, 2004.

Other Papers & Reports:

> —"Female Juvenile Offenders: Failing Systems, Failing Outcomes," Fall, 2004.
>
> —"The Latina Faculty Experience in the Texas State University System," Fall, 2003.
>
> —"Predictors of Non-Invasive Outcomes in Hostage Negotiations," Fall, 2002.

Languages: Proficient in **Spanish**, some **French, German.**

Andrew Baxter Clay

baxter@NYC-law.net

10 Downing Street, Apt. 2T
New York, New York 10014

Office: (212) 555-6800
Residence: (212) 555-8395

Member, State Bar of New York, admitted 2008

EDUCATION

legal   HARVARD LAW SCHOOL, Cambridge, Massachusetts
Juris Doctorate, June 2008
Activities: Editorial Staff, *Journal on Legislation*
Law School Council: Committee to Revive the Practice Court
Ames Moot Court Competition

college   NORTHWESTERN UNIVERSITY, Evanston, Illinois
Bachelor of Arts, History, 2005
Honors: Phi Beta Kappa
Hearst Award (highest History Department GPA)
Thesis: *Police and Policing in Popular Culture and Public Policy*

prep   PHILLIPS EXETER ACADEMY, Exeter, New Hampshire
Honors: Co-Salutatorian
Debate Champion
Captain, Squash Team

EXPERIENCE

legal   ASCHER, ELIASSON & RHEIKHART, New York, New York
Attorney, August 2008–Present
Member of litigation team in $2.1 billion Texoil v. Mutual Assurance bad-faith insurance coverage case. Conducted research to support lead counsel. Prepared and argued motions. Defended depositions. Currently carrying the major responsibility for a multimillion-dollar commercial dispute between a corporate insured and its insurer.

ASCHER, ELIASSON & RHEIKHART, New York, New York
Summer Associate, July–August 2007
Prepared summary judgment motion. Researched and drafted memoranda for litigation matters. Observed depositions. Received permanent offer.

ISHAM, LINCOLN, SWAN & BEALL, Chicago, Illinois
Extern, June–July 2007
Researched and drafted memoranda for insurance defense cases. Received permanent offer.

HIGGS, FLETCHER & MACK, San Diego, California
Summer Clerk, June–August 2006
Researched and drafted memoranda for personal injury and business litigation practice. Drafted settlement conference briefs for attorney malpractice case.

nonlegal   BAUMAN FARMS, Reese, Michigan
Farmer, summers 2003, 2004, 2005
Operated 200-acre farm on profit-sharing basis. Supervised crew. Maintained equipment. Made crop marketing decisions. Earned 100% of tuition.

BARBARA J. DAMLOS

damlos@waltweb.com

1800 Greenwich Street   Cell: (415) 555-6451
San Francisco, CA 94132   Residence: (415) 555-1636

EXPERIENCE   **MISCIAGNA & COLOMBATTO,** San Francisco, California
Partner   1/2005–Present
Insurance defense litigation in the areas of insurance coverage, insurer bad faith, personal injury, and product liability. Drafted appellate writs.

Published opinions:
Bodenhamer v. Superior Ct. (G.A.B.)(2006)178.Cal.App.3d.180
Bodenhamer v. Superior Ct. (St. Paul)(2007)192.Cal.App.3d.1472

Primary responsibility for trial preparation. Assisted lead counsel in four-month trial of insurance bad faith case.

TOLPEGIN, IMAI & TADLOCK, San Francisco, California
Law Clerk   7–12/2004
Directed discovery of toxic tort litigation. Researched and drafted pleading, motions for summary judgment, and discovery requests. While studying for bar.

BIANCO, BRANDI & JONES, San Francisco, California
Summer Associate and Extern   5/2003–5/2004
Researched issues in unfair competition, trade secrets, and product liability. Reviewed personal injury and malpractice cases. While law student.

HANCOCK, ROTHBERT & BUNSHOFT, San Francisco, California
Summer Associate   6–8/2002
Researched legal issues in bankruptcy proceedings, construction actions, and insurance coverage cases involving asbestos-related claims.

HANCOCK, ROTHBERT & BUNSHOFT, San Francisco, California
Paralegal   7/2000–8/2001
Assisted in preparation of two major construction cases for trial.

EDUCATION   **UNIVERSITY OF SAN FRANCISCO SCHOOL OF LAW**
Juris Doctor   2004
Law Review
Semi-Finalist, Advocate of the Year, Moot Court Competition Honors Program
First Place, Oral Advocacy, Moot Court Competition

PUBLICATION   *The Duty of Good Faith—More Than Just a Duty to Defend and Settle Claims,* 14
Western State University L.Rev.209(Fall 2006)

AFFILIATIONS   Member, State Bar of California, admitted 2004
California Trial Lawyers Association
Bar Association of San Francisco

(Please keep this application confidential at this time.)

Marybeth Whitney-Winegrove

600 Quincy Street, #110
Boston, Massachusetts 02125

whitney-winegrove@wallstreeters.net
24 hour private voice/message/text/fax: (617) 555-8311

EXPERIENCE

financial

M. P. Handel & Co., Inc., 2005–Present
Boston, Massachusetts

Institutional Equity Sales Trader, 2007–Present
Service 30 major institutional accounts. Solicit trades, execute trades, develop client relationships, distribute research product, represent investment ideas. Recent concentration has been educating clients on our foreign products, including settlement operations and capital commitment services. Completed intensive research project on international program trading.

Selected to take over the entire account base of a senior partner, a total of 76 accounts. Completed two months advanced training in New York. Currently travel approximately 30 percent to key accounts and company offices in New York, Philadelphia, Washington, Singapore, and London.

Sales Assistant to Research Salesperson, 2005–2007

Assisted in sales and client services related to analysts' reports on 15 selected industries. Included direct client interaction at all levels, planning/hosting/ coordinating meetings and social engagements for institutional investors. Provided administrative and technical support. Coordinated with New York and Washington offices. Retained through several mergers: M. P. Handel, Smythe & Holden, Rowe & Pitman.

prior

Lanier Business Products, Inc.
Chicago, Illinois
Senior Sales Representative, Corporate Accounts
Top producer

Weather Tamer, Inc.
Chicago, Illinois
Assistant Marketing Director

Huntington Industries, Inc.
Chicago, Illinois
Cost Analyst

Bullocks Wilshire
Los Angeles, California
Department Manager

EDUCATION

M.B.A., Finance, Boston University, 2003
B.S., Fashion Retailing, Institute of Design, Chicago, 1998

CREDENTIALS

NASD Series 7 (Series 63 pending)

E. Edleff Schwaab

mr.finance@telnet.com
1250-F Piccadilly Place, White Plains, New York 10601
(914) 555-5820 (home), (800) 555-2406 (office)

EDUCATION	NEW YORK UNIVERSITY, New York, New York	
	M.B.A., Finance, *summa cum laude*	2003
	SYRACUSE UNIVERSITY, Syracuse, New York	
	B.S., Accounting, *magna cum laude*	2000

CREDENTIAL

CFA Candidate
Level I (passed) — 2009
Level II (results pending) — 2010
Level III (anticipated) — 2011

EXPERIENCE

MAHAN, ROMANSKI & O'CONNOR, LPC, New York, New York
Portfolio Co-Manager/Securities Analyst　　　　2010–Present

Co-manage a publicly traded, diversified high-growth mutual fund. Develop the original investment strategy, prepared marketing material, and selected investments for the fund. Performance has led to an eightfold increase in assets under management in the fund to $18 million in the first 7 months. This fund is currently performing third out of 86 high-yield funds as ranked by Lipper.

Also prepare general investment analysis for this firm, which has $1 billion total assets under management. Conduct fundamental research, communicate with management and sell-side analysts, and assess economic and industry trends. Selected and monitor investments in the following sectors: banks, S&Ls, insurance, airlines, aerospace, defense, machinery and equipment, diversified companies, convertible bonds, and high-yield bonds.

EMPIRE FINANCE SAVINGS BANK, Riverhead, New York
Senior Investment Analyst　　　　2008–2009

Co-managed $100 million high-yield bond portfolio. Recommended investment decisions. Prepared written and oral presentations to CFO, CEO, and chairman on strategies and ideas. Sole liaison to management of companies under investment, sell-side analysts, and traders.

TPFM & C (a Towers Perrin Co.), New York, New York
Senior Financial Analyst　　　　2003–2008

Developed models, projected cash flows, and valued a range of potential mergers, acquisitions, divestitures, LBOs, and alternate capital structures. Developed and analyzed long-range financial and business plans.

Developed methodologies and financial models to analyze 9 acquisitions and 9 divestitures worth over $1.5 billion, which were approved and consummated according to plans.

ASHLAND OIL, Pittsburgh, Pennsylvania
Senior Financial Budget Analyst　　　　2000–2001

Developed, analyzed, and interpreted corporate operating and capital budgets. Supervised 3 financial analysts.

ACTIVITIES

Competent Toastmaster (CTM), Toastmasters International
New York Marathon (last 8 years)

ANDREA TIPTON
(SAG, AFTRA)

Frederick & Templeton Agency, Inc.
6608 Hollywood Boulevard, Hollywood, CA 90028
(213) 555-8506 {in New York call (212) 555-6100}
info@FTA.com

DATA

Height: 5'7"	Hair: Blond	Ages: 20–25
Weight: 115	Eyes: Blue	Lang: Italian, Polish, Greek

FILM

Transformers II	Waitress	Michael Bay, Dir./Dreamworks
Zelda	Zelda	Paul Scott Reuter, Dir./NYU Student Film
Bye Bye Budapest	Mrs. Borbas	Margeaux Wasommer, Dir./WSU Student Film

THEATRE

The Snow Queen	Snow Queen	Long Beach Players/Long Beach
		Deborah La Vine, Dir.

"A visual delight—a female Mr. Spock," Heffley, L.A. Times
"A beautiful, regal Snow Queen," Warfield, Drama-Logue

The Woolgatherer	Rose	New Studio Theatre/Detroit
A Midsummer Night's Dream	Titania	Mullady Theatre/Chicago
Uncommon Women	Rita	Mullady Theatre/Chicago
Lysistrata	Corinthian	Mullady Theatre/Chicago
Rattlesnake in a Cooler	Ellen	Detroit Repertory/Detroit
Who Killed Richard Cory	Mistress	4th St. Playhouse/Royal Oak, MI
Quail Southwest	Kerra	4th St. Playhouse/Royal Oak, MI
The Late George Apley	Lydia	Henry Ford Theatre/Dearborn

COMMERCIALS

List upon request (20+)

STANDUP COMEDY

At My Place	2008	Santa Monica, CA
Igby's Comedy Cabaret	2008	Los Angeles, CA

TRAINING

The Groundlings	Improv	Los Angeles, CA
Judy Carter	Standup Comedy	Los Angeles, CA
Greg Dean	Standup Comedy	Los Angeles, CA
Lawrence Parke	Scene Study	Los Angeles, CA
Loyola University	B.A., Drama, 2006	Chicago, IL, and Rome, Italy
Lodz Film School	Acting	Lodz, Poland
Kosciusko Foundation	Acting	Krakow, Poland

SKILLS

Languages (see above). Horseback riding (English & Western). SCUBA (NAUI certified). Motorcycle riding. Classical piano. Dance (ballet, modern, ballroom).

Bruce Nolin

4366 Monroe Avenue, #107
Studio City, California 91604

answerman@filmtrivia.com
24-hr cell/txt/pager: (818) 555-0575

PRODUCER/CO-PRODUCER/UNIT DIRECTOR

STRENGTHS

- Twelve years in television—great record for on-time and on-budget
- Good communicator with writers, talent, crew, production and post-production
- Strong on directing/shooting inserts and second-unit filming

CREDITS

Virtual High School (New Syndicated Series), The Arthur Company, 2010–Present
  Position: Producer
  Executive Producer: Burton Armus

All Monica-All the Time (A&E), Unscripted Improv, 2008–2009
  Position: Associate Producer
  Executive Producers: Tom and Dick Smothers—Producer: Ken Kragen

Jenny McCarthy's Closet Tapes (Playboy), BRB Productions/Pip Pictures, 2007
  Position: Production Manager
  Executive Producer: Steve Binder—Production Executive: Howard Malley

No Diets Needed (USA for Africa), Malley-Golin Productions, 2005
  Position: Stage Manager
  Executive Producer: Steve Binder—Producers: Craig Golin, Howard Malley

Knight Rider II (NBC Series), Universal Television, 2004–2006
  Position: Associate Producer
  Supervising Producers: Burton Armus, Bruce Landsbury

Simon & Simon (CBS Series), Universal Television, 2002–2004
  Position: Assistant Associate Producer
  Executive Producer: Phil DeGuere—Producer: Richard Chapman

Legends of the West (ABC Special), Marble Arch Productions, 2001
  Position: Production Coordinator
  Producer: Eric Lieber

The Gambler (CBS Movie of the Week), Kenny Rogers Productions, 2000
  Position: Production Coordinator
  Producer: Ken Kragen

The Lily Tomlin Show (NBC Special), Tomlin Productions, 1999
  Position: Production Coordinator
  Producer: Rocco Urbisci

EDUCATION

Premed, University of California, Los Angeles

Marta Paulos

Montreal
Canada

> **"I like snakes; they're flexible and
> come in all colors."**   *—Botero*

Marta Paulos is a Montreal artist known for her sculptures of animals and plants, all of which she calls paintings. Her brightly colored representations exhibit a pervasive sense of humor and a strong sense of the unusual in the mundane. The emotive impact of her works is initially humorous, hiding a more concealed cynicism that adds a depth unknown to many young artists.

A full decade of formal study behind her, Ms. Paulos is working in the tradition of American and Mexican naïve and primitive art. Secondary influences include Flemish portraiture and Italian Renaissance painting.

Ms. Paulos produces unavoidable, interesting sculptures of cacti, people, dogs, snakes, and other animals, and has recently begun to produce a series of houses. Having focused on nearly life-size pieces, she is now moving toward developing arrangements of her independent characters into total environments.

With five years of serious exhibitions, Ms. Paulos is an emerging and prolific artist, and has already won the prestigious Pierce Award for one of her dog sculptures, a yellow pit bull with a snake in his mouth. She has pockets of aficionados throughout Canada and the United States, shows regularly in New York, and is just now beginning to attract the attention of serious collectors.

As a contemporary artist, Ms. Paulos is refreshingly accessible. See her now at the Lumina Gallery, Quebec City, P.Q. (418) 555-0194.

Robertson & Associates, LPC

Attorneys-at-Law
3810 Melrose Place, Suite 1500
Los Angeles, California 90029
(213) 555-4964 or (213) 555-1713
www.robertsonlawyers.com

Nathaniel A. Robertson
BIOGRAPHY

Nathaniel A. Robertson is a graduate of Stanford University and the University of California at Berkeley (Boalt Hall) School of Law. He is a member of the ABA, the NBA, and the CBA, and is licensed to practice before all California State Courts, Federal District Court, and the U.S. Court of Appeals. Mr. Robertson is well known in legal and business circles in both Northern and Southern California. He has been described by at least one media source as a "major force in West Coast litigation" (Law Week).

Mr. Robertson is currently the principal of Robertson & Associates, LPC, a law firm specializing in legal research and representation concerning matters of securities, Sarbanes Oxley, banking, commercial credit, tax law, general business and contract litigation, professional liability, product liability, appellate services, and related services such as negotiations, advocacy memoranda, and representation to tax, government, or regulatory authorities.

In addition to heading his law practice, Mr. Robertson serves as a private consultant on commercial credit and investment contracts. He provides transaction advisory services, structuring, and oversight for a wide range of financial and joint-venture agreements. This includes projects for such institutions as the European Industrial Development Bank and the Arbuckle Consulting Group (the renowned Southern California venture capital firm).

Prior to starting his firm, Mr. Robertson was the founder and executive director of the Western Legal Research Institute at Stanford for seven years. WLRI is a legal think tank and support firm providing quality research, writing, and analysis to private practitioners, corporate counsel, and attorneys in government. Mr. Robertson built a team of dynamic young attorneys around this new concept, and this "law firm's law firm" gained quick recognition as both innovative and highly resourceful. WLRI has continued to grow and has been touted as the model of a new breed of legal services firm.

WLRI provides litigation, research, and analysis in the areas of administrative law, automobile injury, banking, civil procedure, civil rights, commercial law and bankruptcy, constitutional law, contracts, corporate law and antitrust, criminal law and procedure, eminent domain, energy, environmental law, family law, labor law, pension benefits, copyright and trademark, personal injury, product liability, real property, securities, torts, trusts, wills and estates, and workers' compensation.

Mr. Robertson's earlier career spans assignments as research attorney for the California Supreme Court and research clerk/fellow/extern for Public Advocates, Inc., Honorable Justice Frank M. Newman, Pacific Gas and Electric Corporation, National Aeronautics and Space Administration, Legal Aid Society of Alameda County, and the U.S. House of Representatives Subcommittee on Equal Rights.

Chrystal Ann Horton

c/o S. Watson
2310 Rio Grande Street
Houston, Texas 77040

Cell (24 hr. voice/text/pager):
(610) 555-3215
CH2481@gmail.com

PROFILE

Administrative Assistant

- Career secretary, administrator, front and back office staffperson. Over 12 years in office environments. Extensive computer experience. Can self-train on any application.
- Skilled in all general office functions: writing/editing all types of documents and correspondence, bookkeeping/financial entries/invoicing, general clerical.
- Also skilled as front office and/or executive assistant: screening calls and visitors, routing mail and deliveries, maintaining calendars, and managing travel arrangements.

HISTORY

Gulf Coast Salvage & Recycling
Office Administrator
Duties:

- Handle all administrative, secretarial, and clerical support for plant. Manage large cash fund and accounting records. Prepare weekly/monthly production reports and ledger entries.

Brookstone
Authorizations Representative, Credit Department
Duties:

- Verify credit cards for "no address match" online and telephone orders. Communicate with customers and credit card companies.

Monadnock Building Associates
Administrative Assistant
Duties:

- Receptionist for the management office of this high-rise building. Handle lease administration, accounts receivable ledger, correspondence, and general secretarial.

Latch Management Services
Receptionist
Duties:

- Front desk for this management consulting firm. Requires advanced interpersonal and client relations skills, in addition to general office.

Blue Cross of Texas
Clerk/Customer Service
Duties:

- Third-party liability clerk and customer service representative for Hospital and Professional Liaison Unit, and Correspondence Unit.

EDUCATION

Certificate, Administrative Management Studies, IGT Technical Institute, Tulsa, Oklahoma

DANI S. CHESNEY

3736 Lakeland Avenue
Minneapolis, Minnesota 55422

dsc2010@alumni.colorado.edu
(303) 555-4972

INTERESTS

Editing, Writing, Research
Strengths:
- Technical command of the English language: grammar, syntax, semantics, spelling, punctuation.
- Experience in copyediting and proofreading according to multiple stylebooks, including *The Chicago Manual of Style* and the *APA Handbook*.
- Significant experience in primary research; very resourceful at finding data and developing primary and secondary sources.
- Wide-ranging knowledge of history, politics, culture, and science.

EDUCATION

degrees

University of Colorado, Boulder
B.A., History December 2010
- Graduated magna cum laude
- Thesis: *Cinderella Learned to Fly: An Examination of Women Aviators of WWII*

Shady Side Academy, Pittsburgh, Pennsylvania
Diploma May 2006

activities

National Outdoor Leadership School
Leadership Training Spring 2008
- Baja California survival and ecology trip

University of Pittsburgh, Pennsylvania
Semester at Sea Fall 2007
- Traveled around the world on the U.S.S. Universe

symposia

Writing for New Media scheduled for Spring 2011

Magazine Writers' Symposium Fall 2010

Aspen Writers' Conference Summer 2010

EXPERIENCE

University of Colorado, Boulder
Researcher (senior research project) 2009–2010
- Collected data from across the country on women aviators of WWII. Researched primary and secondary materials in USAF National Archives and other government sources.
- Filed three Freedom of Information Act (FIA) requests and followed them through to conclusion.
- Found and interviewed women veterans. Visited USAF Academy to record views of women cadets today.
- Wrote 80-page academic thesis.

University of Colorado, Boulder
Instructor's Assistant, "Astrology 121 Field Study, Western Skies" Fall 2009

University Hill Elementary School, Boulder, Colorado
Tutor, Reading and Writing Fall 2009

TRAVEL

Bicycled in New Zealand; traveled in Australia, Thailand Spring 2011

Traveled in Europe; bicycled in England, Scotland, Ireland Spring 2009

Kayaked in Baja California Summer 2007

ERNIE

Alley #3
Corner of Market & Broadway
Megaopolis, New York 10012

OBJECTIVE

Long-term position as Housecat

QUALIFICATIONS

- Omnivorous. Strong rodent-control capabilities.
- Excellent nonverbal communication skills. Highly developed purring mechanism.
- Affectionate. Adaptable. Rare feline willingness to follow established guidelines.
- Proven stud potential.

EXPERIENCE

BARNCAT, Westchester Estate, New York   March 2008–May 2010

Ensured day-to-day rodent and small animal control for two-story, 35,000 sq.ft. horse stables and barn.

- Captured and consumed average of over 3 rodents per day.
- Achieved 37 percent reduction in barn swallow population.
- Awarded feline leukemia inoculation after 1 month of service.
- Earned in-house privileges for outstanding service and deportment after only 2 months on the job!

ALLEYCAT, Wilshire Boulevard, Los Angeles, California   November 2006–February 2008

Successfully maintained territorial boundaries of 4 sq. block area in notoriously competitive and dangerous location. Developed high degree of proficiency in urban survival, hunting, and scavenging skills.

- Honored by co-cats for consistent expertise in maneuvering safely and adroitly through heavy skateboard, auto, and roller-skate traffic.
- Known sire of at least 77 feline liters over a 9-month period.
- Attracted attention of wealthy tourist and earned free ride to Westchester County estate!

EDUCATION

Certificate, Feline Deportment   January 2007
TOM & JERRY ASSOCIATES, Hollywood, California
(1-year intensive with Tom of famed "Tom & Jerry" partnership)
High Honors

REFERENCES

Enthusiastic recommendations provided upon request.

CALIDA L. COLEMAN

7320 Shorepoint Drive
Detroit, Michigan 48220
CLC@kidzplace.org
(313) 555-6210

EDUCATION

<u>Clinton Elementary School</u>, Detroit, Michigan, 2007 to Present
GPA: 3.75/4.0
Study/learn complicated 5th grade materials:

- math
- reading
- social studies
- science
- English
- studio art

Accomplishments:
Maintain outstanding attendance and conduct.
Photo was selected to appear in school promotional literature.

<u>Plymouth Day Care School</u>, Detroit, Michigan, 2007
Completed rigorous program of kindergarten studies. Mastered phonics foundations and socialization skills. Performed in Christmas and Easter programs.

ACTIVITIES

<u>Clinton School Players</u>

- Shrek to the Rescue–May 2010—Princess Fiona
  One of the lead characters. Performed two solo songs.

- Hello Dolly–May 2009—Judge
  Speaking and tap dancing role.

- The Lion King–May 2008—Zazu
  Speaking role with two solo songs.

- Peter Pan–May 2007—Cast
  Chorus member.

<u>Music</u>

- Piano lessons since 2008, with continuing progress to more complex pieces by Bach, Beethoven, Chopin, Czerny, Liszt and others.

INTERESTS

Mathematics, reading, writing stories, singing, dancing, performing, and my continuing research on American amusement parks.

15 How to Get Interviews and Plan and Manage a Job Search

A job search is like a game of chess: It has an opening, middle, and an endgame. You use different strategies in each stage, and you watch every moment for an unexpected opportunity to seize and exploit.

First, you must build a strong opening position, creating a network from which to launch multiple attacks on your objective. In the middle, you must keep track of a large volume of possibilities; an error at this point could turn the tide of the game against you. In the endgame, you must sustain your advantage, close in on your target, and win.

First you must make a personal decision to plan and manage your job search aggressively. Decide to commit resources to your job search, especially *time* and *money*. Make sure you have the raw ingredients: a businesslike email address, a professional message on all your phone lines, access to email on a daily basis, an appointment calendar that is failsafe, and a decent place to work. Yes, it is true that you can get a job without any of these things, but it's a heck of a lot easier *with* them.

Even if you decide to use your kitchen table as the "command center" for your job search, you must have access to it; it should be clean and well organized, and the project should not have to compete for your attention with jelly drippings or blaring televisions.

Also, as you begin to get interviews, you will need to have a perfect personal appearance. That means at least one complete outfit, from topcoat to umbrella. Now *is* the time to splurge and buy a new suit of clothes. Pay attention to details and accessories. Do your watch and your shoes fit with your job objective? Do your clothes fit you as you are today? If money is a real problem, borrow the items you need to complete the outfit. You can buy your own "career accessories" after your new job improves your cash flow.

Clothes are far more important than you might believe. They really do need to be *perfect*. It is a good idea to scout the company before your interview to see how people at your level dress, and imitate them. You *can* overdress, so a suit is not always a safe choice. You want to dress like they would dress when the out-of-town big boss comes to visit. And, obviously, there is never a "casual Friday" for jobseekers.

Do not muddle through this project with halfway measures. The result is your future. Look good, and you will feel good and be confident.

Active versus Passive Search and the Hidden Job Market

If you wait for the employer to post an opening for a position, you're going to face massive competition throughout your job search. There will always be dozens if not hundreds or thousands of other people applying for those jobs. Some people do get jobs by applying for posted openings, but remember that, necessarily, dozens *or thousands* of others end up disappointed.

There's a radically different way to look for work, and it's much more effective. Go out and look for a certain *type of job*, whether you see any posted openings or not. You can apply for posted openings, of course, but you don't need to wait for a posting. Approach the company directly, before they can post an opening. Here's why: ***All organizations are always hiring***.

They may not be hiring somebody like you, but they are hiring somebody. When you read about a company laying off thousands of people, they are at that same time hiring people. People die, retire, take maternity leave, go on vacation, refuse to learn a needed new skill, pick a fight with a powerful boss, and so on, creating opportunity everywhere. The company reorganizes jobs and work processes, and needs different people with different skillsets to do those jobs. A business unit is moved from place A to place B, and needed workers refuse to relocate. A process is outsourced to a contractor, creating layoffs at the first company but new hiring in the contractor. All change creates opportunity somewhere. So hiring is going on, all the time, even in a challenging economy.

In fact, this point is even more important in a tight economy. If your local economy has high unemployment, once a job is posted you can bet it is going to draw stiff competition. Lots of those applicants are going to be more experienced than you, better looking than you, better dressed than you, older or younger than you. So in a tight economy it is even more important than ever that you not wait for the job to be posted. Once it's posted, you have to be perfect to get the job.

In fact, a lot of jobs are never advertised at all. The staffing need is filled by someone who is referred by a current employee, or by someone who just happens to be in the right place at the right time. That's your goal: to be in the right place at the right time.

Building a Target List

What type of job do you want? If you know what you want you can go look for it. What industry is most attractive or logical for you? What function will you perform on the job? What title might you hold? This is the minimum definition of a job:

- Industry, such as advertising, or county government, or commercial real estate

- Function, such as accounting, or sales, or customer service

- Title, the name of the job you will seek

Where is the job? What will you wear to work? Who do you report to? How often will you interact with your boss? Will you supervise anyone? What are their titles and functions? How many hours a week would be normal for someone to do this type of job? What skills are required?

This vision of the job you are after should drive your search process. You can have more than one idea at a time, of course. You can be interested in a couple or three different types of jobs simultaneously, but don't go wildly off in all directions at once. It's not effective. You'll need to change your resume for every single target; you'll need different stories to tell in interviews, etc. So restrict your list to one to four targets at a time. If you discover that a target is unattractive or unrealistic, you can drop it and add another one then.

You'll need to get specific about the type of job you're going to seek *even if you're not sure.* Being specific helps you get started, and helps other people help you. So, it's not enough to say you're interested in green business, or you want a job that has to do with the environment. That's not specific enough to drive your actions. You need targets that are this specific:

TARGET

> Industrial level recycling of post-consumer electronics, as in container loads or larger, and global trade in such materials.

With a target that is specific, you can start contacting people. Define one to four specific types of jobs you want, before going further.

Building Lead Lists

Your next task is to build lead lists. It helps if you have specific goals in mind, so you know which leads are likely to be valuable, and which are likely to be long shots. A job lead may be a person you know, a friend of a friend, an online ad, a news item, or even a rumor. Here are the main sources for job leads:

- Networking
- Research
- Job Boards
- Company Web Sites

- Print Media

- Headhunters and Agencies

- Job Fairs

- College Recruiting

Networking is easy. Your targets are everybody you could contact who might know you by name or by reference. They range from alumni of your high school or university; to members of your church, synagogue, mosque, temple, or ashram; to second cousins you haven't seen in years; to all the "friends" you have on your accounts in FaceBook, MySpace, LinkedIn, and so on. They include at least everyone in your family, all your neighbors, all your friends (current and past), everyone who ever went to the same schools as you, all the members of every club or organization to which you belong, every employer or fellow employee of every company at which you have ever worked, and every coach or teacher you've ever had, and *all their friends and acquaintances.* That's a lot of people. For most of us, this is several hundred people, maybe thousands.

It doesn't matter if your contact is as dumb as a post and lives on the other side of the country, either. At all levels, from migrant farm worker to the top echelons of the business elite, some version of personal referral is the number one source of the job lead that results in employment. I will tell you what to do with these lists in a moment.

Next, use **research** to make lists of companies that you would like to contact. If you are interested in working for an environmental remediation engineering firm, find every environmental remediation engineering firm in your area. If you want to work for a conservative think tank in California or Washington, D.C., find *every* conservative think tank in California or Washington, D.C.

You don't need to be an expert at research to do this. Once you can define the type of company you're after, a good research librarian can help you build the list. You pay taxes to support the library, so get in there and get some help. Your college career center may also be able to give you guidance throughout your search. They'll guide you to resources such as www.hoovers.com, or www.zapdata.com, or association directories where you can take an idea and turn it into a list.

So if you have the MegaChem Company of Hoboken, New Jersey, in your sights, use research to turn that one idea into a list of *all companies like it.* Your research librarian can show you how to create a list of every chemical manufacturing plant in New Jersey with over $10,000,000 in sales, for example.

You can search your way to a list of companies, also. Clever combinations of search terms can help you discover firms that match your criteria. Google or Bing "suitcase repair shops" if that is a skill that you possess, and you'll quickly find every one.

Being systematic is the key to success. If you are qualified to be a leasing agent for one commercial real estate office, you are qualified to be a leasing agent for any other one. Oh, and just for the record, do not forget that the majority of new jobs (entry- to executive-level) are created in small- to medium-sized businesses, not Fortune 500 companies. Fortune 500 companies are net destroyers of jobs. So be smart and be open to companies you've never heard of before.

Your list should include all your current employer's competitors, vendors, clients, and venture partners. Just for the record, the most obvious next job for you is at one of your current employer's competitors. And before you give up on your current employer, be sure to look for an attractive assignment in other branches, divisions, or cities. Changing employers is taxing, and you might be able to find exactly what you want somewhere in the far-flung reaches of your own organization.

Needless to say, this list of companies will overlap your list of networking contacts. That is, some of your contacts will work at these companies. That is fine. You will launch multiple attacks on these targeted companies anyway.

––––––––––––

The larger **job boards** have millions of jobs, but they also have many millions of jobseekers. *Do not rely overmuch on job boards.* They should be one of your search methods, but never the only one. Not even the geekiest techie should rely only on Internet job leads.

Some of the large national ones are www.monster.com, www.careerbuilder.com, and www.craigslist.org. There are tons of specialty boards, such as www.allretailjobs.com, www.dice.com (for technical jobs), www.higheredjobs.com (for college and university hiring), and so on. There are high quality boards that focus on a specific state, such as http://jobstar.org/index.php (California). Finally, local job boards serve most cities and towns in the country. For more, see www.weddles.com, which tracks and ranks job sites.

There are two ways to use most of them: either search for posted openings that look attractive to you and apply to them, or post your resume so that employers can find you. Unique words are often the key to getting a call, and remember to find ways to put any unusual words from the posting into the resume that you submit for any job. Change your resume often, so you show up as active. Get that local zip code onto your documents. Consider anonymizing your resume to protect yourself from unwanted and inappropriate contacts. (Review the resume advice on pages 20–21, and page 29 covering these issues.)

The more unusual your skills, such as you are a PE (professional engineer) *and* you speak Pashto, and the more mobile you are (willing to work anywhere in the country, or even the world), the better the job boards work.

Company websites also advertise openings and accept unsolicited resumes. They don't have the traffic that the major national boards have, and that's a good thing! You should *always* drop your resume into company web sites if the company is interesting to you. You have to check back often to view new listings. You should try to site a connection with a current employee. These web sites have a bias designed into the software in favor of employee referrals (because employee referrals are associated with higher quality candidates, higher rates of hire, and longer tenures). In short, employee referrals go to the top of the pile. You can use www.linkedin.com, www.facebook.com, www.plaxo.com, or other social networking sites to see if you have any potential connections (or can get an introduction).

––––––––––––

Print media are not totally dead in the job search. Some of the coolest jobs in the world are posted in the *Economist* every week. Your local newspaper will have new listings every day. Most newspapers now have online ads that duplicate the print version, so this is a hybrid resource really, both print and online. Newspaper ads have been infected with a lot of low quality career "opportunities," however, and to find the real jobs you'll have to sort through bogus offers to pay for your own training and sell unwanted products to your closest friends. On the other hand, if you read them every day, you'll be able to spot the new ads the day they come out.

Industry and trade publications and all types of micromarket media remain good sources of job announcements, especially when employers want to attract a candidate with an existing interest in an area or an industry. So read the ads in publications like *Dogwalkers' Weekly, Down East Backcountry News,* or *Summer Camp & Youth Leadership Monthly.* Newsletters and association organs, both online and print, are a good source of leads for unique jobs in obscure fields.

The newspaper and business magazine media are also great places to get ideas—and to get a feel for economic conditions in your area and in your field. If you read that a company is opening, or doing well, or won a big contract, or their stock is rising, or they're moving a business unit, then you have a job lead of real value. There will be more jobs behind a typical news story than there are behind any job posting you might read, in print or online.

Headhunters and **employment agencies** are a great source of job leads, especially if you have unusual, unique, or obscure skills. The old maxim was "agencies find jobs for people; headhunters find people for jobs."

Retainer headhunters find and vet applicants in the six-figure-and-up range. They work under exclusive contracts. They prefer the term "executive search consultant" over the term "headhunter," although the pejorative connotations of the latter are disappearing. Contingency headhunters are paid only if they make a placement, and they usually do *not* have exclusive requisitions. They place people at all levels, but prefer to place managers, executives, and highly compensated people with rare and valuable skills. All headhunters prefer to place people who are currently employed, have been promoted in the last two or three years, and are willing to move anywhere their next assignment may take them. Since headhunters find people for jobs, unless you happen to perfectly match a headhunter's current searches, she can't do anything for you besides talk to you as a courtesy. To learn more about headhunters, and to find the ones that serve your industry, function, or geographical area, there is one premiere source: Kennedy Information, www.kennedyinfo.com. Their web site also has some very high-quality articles on the job search that can be accessed for free.

Permanent-placement agencies can help you get a job, certainly. The most useful ones specialize, with firm names such as *Bilingual Secretaries Unlimited.* Avoid any agencies that want to charge you, the jobseeker, for finding you a job, testing your skills, or training. If an agency's services are not free to you, walk right back out the door. Temporary agencies can help you pick up some cash while you continue your look for a permanent assignment. For any jobseeker who is clueless about what kind of job he or she might want, a temp agency can be a godsend. They'll send you out on all kinds of assignments, so you can gain exposure to different work environments, different industries, and different tasks. Many temp assignments do result in a permanent placement, known as temp-to-perm, but here's a big warning: Lots of temp workers in America today have become an underclass, working part-time *for years* without benefits and without job security. So be careful that a little adventure doesn't become a lifetime.

If you know any HR managers in your field, ask them what headhunters or agencies they use or can recommend.

Job fairs are a great way to get face to face with real, live recruiters. They can be agonizing and frustrating, as well. Register online, strategize in advance which companies you most want to connect with, arrive there early, dress well, and get ready to be told, over and over again, to apply online. You want to collect everyone's business card—or carefully record their name, title, and email—so you can email them your resume directly, in addition to complying with their application instructions.

Recruiters use job fairs to find hard-to-source people, so don't be discouraged if you walk up to someone's table and he has a large sign behind him: "Nuclear Engineers, Aerosol Engineers, Rocket Scientists, Entomologists, Gypsy Contortionists, Fire Eaters." They also need marketing assistants and public relations interns, so just ask them about opportunities that match your skillset.

College recruiting is a great source of jobs leads, and not just if you're in college. If you've graduated, your career center can continue to help you with leads, referrals, ideas, interview preparation, resume fine tuning, and so on. Most colleges and universities now have lifetime career services, although alumni may have to pay token fees for some types of support. You are probably not going to be able to access on-campus recruiters, but in some cases you may. Ask. It never hurts to ask. And if your university helps keep your career on track, be sure to be a generous donor as your cash flow improves.

Making Contact

Now you have this huge amalgam of leads, ranging from posted openings to old friends. How do you go about *systematically* finding a new position? Obviously, apply to all the posted openings that match your interests, apply online to all the companies that match your interests, but then it is time to design and launch a systematic marketing campaign. One channel targets people, and one channel targets organizations.

For people, email every human being you can obtain an email address for and ask them if they know of any people in the specific industries you've targeted. Here's a great structure for this query: "Hey, Mike, I'm about to graduate from college and I'm thinking about public service jobs. My dream job or internship would be with the United Nations. Who do you know who would know anything about internships at the United Nations?"

Here's a model for someone older: "Hello, Jesse. I've found myself on the job market due to a downsizing. I guess that happened to a lot of people. Anyway, I'm interested in making a shift from construction to something in health care. Who do you know who would know anything about healthcare, either the financial and administrative side, or the clinical side?"

To paraphrase former Chicago Mayor Daley, "Email early and email often." Build an email list of friends and friends-of-friends, and let them all know you're on the market and what you're after. Consider blogging your job search or covering it daily on your social networking sites. Tell everybody what kind of an opportunity you're seeking, and ask them if they have any ideas or advice for you. Ask them to keep an ear out for any information that might be of interest to you in your search. Be sure to let them know you'll be emailing them from time to time during your job search, and that if they don't have any information you'll understand if they're too busy to respond.

It is also a good idea to send them a copy of your resume. Ask them if they have any suggestions for improving it, and invite them to forward it to anyone who might be interested, or anyone they might know in certain industries. If you have any champions out there, you may be able to persuade them to send your resume to all their high quality contacts, with a note like this, "John, this is a high quality individual who happens to be on the market. I've known this guy for years, and I can tell you he's a strong performer, with high integrity, the kind of person who is a long-term asset to an organization. If you can use him, I'll vouch for him. If not, feel free to send this on to anyone you can think of."

One thing you do not do is ask them if they have any job openings where they work. If they do, they'll tell you. Do not ask your contacts for a job; ask for ideas, advice, leads, information, and referrals. This is called "lowering the ante." Asking them for a job puts them on the spot. It makes them say no to you, and nobody wants to say no. It's human nature to want to help someone, so ask them for something they can give you, such as ideas and advice. When you lower the ante, your contact is genuinely relieved, and that relief translates into a greater willingness to help you with a meeting or a viable job lead. You can ask them "Do you know anybody who is hiring in accounting right now? Any companies with expansion plans or staffing needs?" If their own company is hiring, and they don't think you're a dud, they'll tell you.

Listen to the advice you get as you use this system. If everyone is saying the same thing, then it's probably true. So if everyone tells you you need to move to New York, or learn Tagalog, or start at the entry level, or grow a personality, then that's advice you're going to have to consider probably valid.

With organizations that you've identified as good potential places to work, obviously you apply to any openings on their recruiting web site, and you post your resume if there is a process to do so. But then you start studying their web site in greater detail. What actual human beings are identified on the web site, anywhere? Obviously you also run a search on the company's name and the names of its main products and services, which can lead to names of humans and email addresses. Here's something that works, especially with smaller organizations: Run a search on the company's raw URL (for example, "roundtire.com" to find everyone with email addresses that end in "roundtire.com").

Go to LinkedIn and see if the company's profile is there, or who you might know or be able to connect to who has ever worked there. If you are systematic and diligent, you will be able to come up with dozens or hundreds of emails for most companies.

Then, write to any and all of these email addresses, these people you don't even know, and ask them this simple question: "I am interested in working for your company, and my expertise is [name something specific]. Who would I talk to about that? Who would handle that type of thing?" Don't provide a resume, although you might include just a hint about yourself. Most contacts will either ignore you or tell you to "apply online," which you've already done, but some of them are going to respond with info like this: "Our Asian Sales Rep is Dani DeLong, and she can be reached at (212) 555-2941 or dani@slingshot.com. Good luck!"

The Elevator Speech

As you approach your contacts who do not personally know you, you will need a twenty-second introduction, also known as an elevator speech. If you got on the elevator with a senior officer in a company, what could you tell them about you that would matter, in the course of going up or down a few floors? That's an elevator speech. So you reach a stranger on the phone, what do you say? Here are two examples:

"I am a college student majoring in psychology. I am interested in sports administration. I am on several campus committees devoted to promoting and producing sporting events, both intercollegiate and intramural. My ultimate goal would be to land in sports marketing and sponsorship sales, but I am also interested in other areas. I got your name from the alumni office, and I wonder if you would have a moment to speak with me about the sports business."

———

"I am an MBA student interested in operations management. My experience to date has emphasized matrix- and liaison-management of offshore manufacturing plants, working with both joint-venture and contracting structures and wholly-owned offshore units. I speak Spanish fluently, and have picked up a little Chinese and Gaelic. My career interest is global manufacturing and anything to do with synchronization of non-co-located corporate operations, such as engineering on one continent and production on another. I'm calling because I understand your company has operations on Taiwan."

Write out an elevator speech now. You're going to need it.

"We're Not Hiring" and Other Common Objections

If a targeted employer says they are not hiring, you have three options. Your most bold option is to ask them if you could stop by to say hello, anyway. Say something like "Even if you don't need anyone now, I'd like you to know what I have to offer, in case something opens up in the future. A moment of your time now could save you a lot of trouble later on in case you do have an unexpected staffing change. I could just stop by, give you a chance to meet me, and I'll be on my way."

Remember, people have to meet you to hire you, and you need to get out there and meet some people on the thinnest pretexts. Sitting around sending emails is not meeting people.

Alternately, you can ask for an informational interview. This is most apt if you are a career changer *and* charming, or a young person fresh out of school. You can do this with friends and strangers alike. "Actually, I'm very curious about this field, and wonder if you'd be willing to answer a few questions for me about it, either in person or via email." If they hold you to email, you can only ask two or three questions. If you get into their office, you can ask a lot more. Here're seven questions to ask in an information interview format:

1. How did you get into this?

2. What kind of preparation is typical to get into this? Is that really required, or just the typical approach?

3. What was different from what you expected? What was the biggest surprise when you went into this? Any myths you want to shatter for me?

4. Who else does this? What other companies? Who else should I be talking to?

5. What ensures continued advancement?

6. What is the typical career path out of this position or field? What does this prepare you for next? For example, What's next for you?

7. What advice do you have for someone like me?

And maybe if you are there in the office and the meeting is going well, an eighth question could be about salary, but be careful. If you ask about salary, don't ask about their salary or salaries at their company. Ask, "What could a person expect to make in a position like this?" Or, "What would be a typical salary industry wide for a position like this?"

Thirdly, if they say they are not hiring, you can ask them for a referral. "Do you know of other divisions of your company, or other departments, that might be hiring now?" If they say "no," then push on with this question: "Do you know of other companies that might be hiring? Have you heard of anyone expanding or adding staff?"

The fact that a company claims it is not hiring has no bearing on its potential value to your job search. In fact, as you network out past your closest friends, you will constantly run into four objections. Here they are, with suggested responses:

"We're not hiring."

- "That's okay. I'm not applying for a job with you anyway. I am interested in your advice."

- "That's okay. I'm not in any hurry. I just wanted you to know what I have to offer in case something opens up later."

- "That's okay. I just wanted to know if you would take a look at my resume and give me any advice, ideas, leads, or referrals that come to mind."

- "That's okay. Perhaps you can think of someone else who might be interested right now in what I have to offer. Your referral could be appreciated by both of us."

"I'm too busy."

- "This'll only take a moment."

- "Yeah. I heard you guys were pretty successful right now" (then, *stop speaking*, no matter how long the silence).

- "I'd be happy to meet you early, late, during lunch, even after work. What's best for you?"

- "What's a better time for me to reach you?"

"Send me your resume."

- "Well, let me tell you what's on it. I'm the one who—" Then give them your elevator speech.

- "What's your email? I'll email it to you while we are speaking."

- "I'll bring it to the meeting. What's a good time for you?"

"I'm not the person you should be talking to," OR, the dreaded "just apply online."

- "But I'm not applying for a job. I got your name from _____. She said you were quite knowledgeable about this field. I just want to know if you would have a moment to share with me any advice, ideas, leads, and referrals."

- "Actually, I'm going to be applying through 'official' channels, as well, but I wondered if you could give me a little inside information."

- "Who should I be talking to about this? I appreciate the referral."

Interviewing

Once you start to get interviews for real openings, you'll need to be careful to research the company thoroughly. Recruiters tell me the most disappointing interviews they ever conduct are with people who have a desirable skillset, but who were too lazy or disinterested or unskilled to investigate the company prior to sitting down for the interview. *Interviews are hard to get.* Make each one count by doing your homework before you get to the appointment.

Dress perfectly. Arrive at the office in question exactly five minutes early. No earlier, and no later. You may need to be on site much earlier than that in order to make sure you are at the right place exactly five minutes early. Be nice to support staff! They are spying on you from the time you turn into the parking lot or step in the door.

Have a set of hero stories prepared in advance. You need five to fifteen stories about when you were outstanding, a real life saver, *a hero*, in your past performance. If you're young, school stories are acceptable. All stories you tell should have these facets: (a) they are true, (b) you are the author or agent for the central action, (c) the outcome was positive. If I ask you to tell me about your greatest failure, you'd better tell me about a failure that had a happy outcome after all. Either you learned something, or you found the silver lining in the cloud, or the event led to changes that were beneficial for all.

Come into the meeting with five to seven points you want to make, and if these points don't come up automatically, you start to make them come up yourself.

Be ready to address each of these prompts:

- Tell me about yourself.

- What are your strengths?

- Weaknesses?

- Where do you see yourself in five or ten years?

- Tell me about your boss. Did you get along well with her?

- What would your former supervisor say about you?

- Why did you leave each position?

- Give me five reasons why I should hire you.

Be ready for behavioral interview questions when the employer asks you explicitly to tell her stories about prior work experiences. There are thousands of these, but they tend to follow the same basic structure. Here are some common ones:

- Tell me about a time when you had an impossible assignment. What did you do, and how did that work out?

- Tell me about a time when you had a teammate who wasn't pulling his weight. What did you do and how did that go?

- Tell me about a time when you had to train someone.

- Tell me about a time when you had a problem with a boss or supervisor.

- Tell me about a time when you observed unethical behavior of a colleague. What did you do about that? What was the outcome?

- Tell me about a time when you dealt with a really difficult customer or client. What happened?

Behavioral interviewing questions are the norm, today, so be ready for them.

At some point they're going to ask you if you have any questions of them, and you'd better have some. If you can't think of anything else, ask these:

- What happened to the last person to hold this position?

- If I do a really good job for you, what would that look like? What would you consider outstanding performance in this position?

- How am I stacking up against your hiring criteria? Do you think I could do this job?

- How many people are you interviewing? When do you think you'll be making a decision? What's next in the process for me?

The hiring cycle at some companies is longer than you could imagine. The causes for the delays will be invisible to you, and most likely have nothing to do with you. A boss may be out of town, there may be a moratorium on hiring, they may be redesigning the job description, and so on. If you haven't heard from them in some time, send a continuing interest email. Keep it simple, but just don't go away. You can say something like this: "I haven't heard from you in some time, and I remain interested in the position of marketing director. As soon as you are ready to proceed with the hiring process, I am ready as well. I've continued to investigate the company, and the more I find out the more I think it could be a great fit."

Don't hesitate to apply late to old postings and tickle inactive connections every couple of weeks, *until they ask you to stop.* Even if they have placed someone in the position, sometimes that person does not work out, and your application or your tickle arrives just as that becomes apparent.

Don't worry about not being first choice. The first choice candidate often is everybody's first choice. She has multiple offers, and declines the company's invitation to employment. The second choice person did very well in the first interview, but that was the result of great career coaching. By the third interview she told an ethnic joke, ordered wine at lunch, and pretended to wipe her nose on the boss's tie. The third choice person thought his spouse would be excited by the move to Manhattan (either New York or Kansas, it doesn't matter), but as the reality looked eminent, she insisted he withdraw his candidacy. The fourth choice person lied on her resume, and so she's out. The fifth choice person got some other job by the time they called him back. The sixth choice person was actually hired, and then she failed the drug test. Something about a vacation in Jamaica, but who cares? You're still in the running, checking in every two weeks or so. Got it?

In the event that they tell you there's no match, *be very gracious.* I've had many clients get call backs from companies. After they were declined for one position they were later hired for a different position. Just say something like this: "Well, I'm sorry this wasn't a match, because I really liked this company and all the people I've met in the interviews. I'd be proud to work for this organization. Should anything open up that might be a better fit, I hope you'll keep me in mind. And if I can do anything for you at all, just let me know." That's a winner's response to losing a hiring decision.

Thank-You Notes

After every interview, do two things:

First, write down what happened, with attention to the interviewer's key concerns. For example, the last person to hold the job may have been dynamite at organization and follow-through, but lousy at dealing with irate clients on the phone. So the hiring authority's key motivator may be your customer service skills. You will need detailed notes to remember these keys as you continue to have a large volume of interviews and contacts.

Then, *that very same day,* write a short, sincere thank-you note to each person you met with, and get it into the mail the same day. In high tech or when dealing with a young interviewer, you can email a thank-you note, but in all other cases it should still be a note in the mail. Your interviewer will be most favorably impressed to receive this promptly. For most positions a bland, business-like card is fine, no flowers or cutesy designs. Neat handwriting is okay, but running the card through a printer is better. For senior people, a thank-you note printed on monarch-sized stationery is impressive.

Another use of a follow-up letter is to address some issue brought up in the interview, or to recoup from some faux pas. If the interviewer thought you lacked direct outside sales experience, this might be a good time to drive home that you were the largest-selling cookie monster the Girl Scouts ever had in the state of Illinois. I think you get the picture.

Organizing and Managing the Search Project

Now that you have some understanding of what you will be doing in your job search, you can see that this is a lot of detail to manage. You will have to track and control this large project, with hundreds or thousands of potential contacts. You will soon find that John is out of town, Lara cannot come to the phone right now, Justin is not the one you should talk to after all, and so on.

I don't care whether you use 5 x 8 cards, lists and lists of notes, a robust sales management software tool like ACT! or CRM, or an online solution like www.jibberjobber.com, you need to be able to follow through precisely. If you don't tickle with an email or phone call when you promise, you're not going to get a job. Remember, you will have hundreds of active contacts going at the same time.

Set quantified goals for new applications each week; follow-ups do not count. A goal of as few as ten new applications per week will soon snowball into a rolling mass of details and follow-up tasks. You must set an ambitious goal for new applications, or you will soon find yourself busy as heck with nothing really going on. You will think things are going great, but your job search could start to wind down before you get any offers. **You must track new contacts every week, and ten is a minimum.**

Take every Friday afternoon off from your job search, but set part of every Sunday to review the last week and to plan the next one. If you have not met your quota for the week, you can respond to some postings on Sunday. If possible, meet with some fellow seekers on Sunday evening for an iced tea or a beer, and honestly share how your week has gone. These informal job clubs are proven very effective at shortening your job search.

I once worked with a gentleman leaving the Air Force who formed such a job club with three of his friends. I wrote his resume and his three friends copied the style perfectly. They each read one get-a-job book every week and reported on it to the others. Their searches were as professionally thought out and well managed as any I have ever witnessed. Their group served as a crucible for ideas and a place to share the ups and downs of the job search process. Job clubs work.

By the way, this is not meant to be a comprehensive job-search guide, just a primer. For more information see my *How to Get Any Job: Life Launch and Re-Launch for Everyone Under 30.*

Once You Start to Get Offers

One you start to get offers, no matter what, do not stop sending out new applications. Meet your quota for new applications right up until the day you start your new job. If you find yourself in the hospital in a full-body cast during your job search, *I want you to send out a minimum of ten new applications per week.*

If you get an offer, make sure it is a firm offer. Ask point blank, "Are you offering me the position?" Define the terms of employment, at a minimum, title, compensation, and start date. If you have a firm offer for the job you really want, accept it and get something in writing before you leave.

It is perfectly within bounds to say you need some time to consider the offer. Be sure the offer stands, by saying something as explicit as this: "I'd like to sleep on this and get back to you with a firm answer by four P.M. tomorrow. Is that acceptable?" Or, "I'd like to discuss this with my spouse and my accountant. I think I can get that done in three days. Can I let you know my answer by Friday noon?"

If the position is not right for you, decline it. You learned a lot in applying for it, and you can use that experience in your continuing search for a position that *is* right for you.

Salary Negotiations

Employers expect you to negotiate for salary. It is important for women, in particular, to negotiate for salary because of research that shows that a significant part of the gender-based wage gap is a result of the fact that more men negotiate than women. Women are equally effective at negotiating, but are less likely to negotiate. For more on this, see *Women Don't Ask: The High Cost of Avoiding Negotiation* by Linda Babcock and Sara Laschever.

There are two parts to salary negotiations: knowledge of the market value for the position in question, and negotiating technique. You need to know how much it will cost the company to hire someone to fill the position *if they don't hire you*. That's the market value for the position. Salary surveys can skew a little high, but you should know what they say about the type of position you're after and the region of the country where you will be working. Remember, a graphic artist in Chicago is going to earn more than a graphic artist in Des Moines. Here are some sources of salary information: job ads that list a salary or range, www.salary.com, http://jobstar.org, www.salaryexpert.com, www.payscale.com, and any industry or professional association you belong to will publish an annual salary survey.

Technique is easy. First, you need to know the three rules of *all* negotiations:

1. Never negotiate until the other person is ready to buy, which for employment matters means, *never negotiate until they actually offer you the job.*

2. The first person to name an exact figure has lost competitive advantage.

3. If you can't walk away from the deal, you're not negotiating, you're begging.

So, to delay negotiations until you get to the job offer stage, I offer you the following scripts. Some are a tad aggressive, but I think you'll get the gist of the technique.

BOSS OR RECRUITER: "What's it going to take to bring you on board, in terms of salary?"

YOU: "Salary is not really my first concern. I'm more interested in the people I'll be working with, the specific tasks I'll be working on, and getting a feel for the job." Then ask a question about one of those topics.

BOSS OR RECRUITER: "Gosh, I guess I never got a clear answer about this, but what are your salary requirements?"

YOU: "From what I've researched, salary seems to be all over the map for a position like this, ranging from $40,000 to $86,000! Will this job fall within that range?"

BOSS OR RECRUITER: "Yes."

YOU: "Great." Then ask an unrelated question.

BOSS OR RECRUITER: "What kind of a salary do expect?"

YOU: "I'm sure you have a salary range for this position. Do you mind sharing that with me?" Then, no matter what she says, you say, "Well, we're in the same ballpark. As long as you can make a competitive offer I'm sure this won't be a problem for us."

If they're *way* off your target, you say, "Well, that seems a little low for what I know I could do for you, but I really like the job and the people I've met so far. I'm sure we can work this out if you decide I'm the right person for the job."

By the way, give them a chance to fall in love with you. I had a management-level client who got desperate and started applying for any job she thought she could perform. She went into a company to talk about a $42,000-a-year admin job, and came out with a $72,000-a-year job with strategic responsibilities. This is especially possible in smaller companies.

When you get to the offer and it is time to actually negotiate, use win-win language. Here's a softball that will get you money: "You know, I was hoping for more compensation than this. What can we do?" No one will get upset if you ask this in a polite way. *Everyone, for every job*, should be willing to ask this.

If they start you low, you'll never get caught up. For a white paper on salary negotiations, just ask me: don@donaldasher.com. I'll send it to you.

Psychology of a Job Search

There is a certain pattern to the emotional life of a jobseeker: He will experience some **identity loss** right away and may reconsider his value as a human being. Americans are particularly bad about over-identifying with their careers. To combat this, focus on your family life and your past successes, and remind yourself that you will have a work life again. Take time to be with your kids. Seek out and rediscover your friendships, which have an emotional as well as practical impact on the success of your job search. Work on your physical fitness while you have the time, and consider finally learning to play guitar, or whatever, to give you outlets besides job search, job search, job search.

In the first stages of her search, a jobseeker may be overconfident and think that this won't take very long at all. She'll be in **denial** about how long this search might last, how much this process may cost, and what she may have to do that is unpleasant or uncomfortable. She may even feel pretty good about all the new possibilities available. Novice jobseekers vastly overestimate their value and attractiveness, and underestimate the competition.

This lasts until the first time the jobseeker doesn't get a job he thinks he should have gotten. He is shocked at the number of other well-qualified candidates, the pickiness and pettiness of some employers, the rude behavior of recruiters, and the unfamiliar and sometimes demeaning gyrations the job-search process demands of him. Then the jobseeker gets in touch with his **anger**.

Anger is a normal response, but dwelling in anger is very dangerous. *Anger can double the duration of your job search.* One can get over it by having realistic expectations, by deciding to move on from whatever resentments one may have about the old employer, and by anger- and stress-management techniques such as exercise, well-planned leisure activities, family support, a carefully maintained daily-living routine, and counseling.

Then, if a search proves difficult, expensive, and time consuming, the jobseeker may go into a period of **depression.** *Depression can double the duration of your job search.* The important thing to remember is that it is perfectly normal to be depressed under these circumstances. But depression is energy sapping, and you need your energy. Treat short-term depression as normal, but any prolonged period of depression should be treated by a professional therapist. Whether you seek outside help or not, be sure to pursue known remedies: physical exercise, relaxation exercise, bright lighting, volunteering, well-planned leisure activities, family support, religious practice, careful attention to personal grooming, a light and varied diet, and a carefully maintained daily routine.

Even the most hard-driving, Type-A manager will experience these psychological impacts of a job search. With luck and attention to the issue, they will be both brief and mild.

The final state, emotionally, is a **new norm**; that is, the jobseeker now views her job search as her normal life, in effect, *her new job.* In this stage, she can take satisfaction in doing her job search well. She learns about job-search techniques the same way she'd learn about any new set of tasks required by her job, breaks up her job-search projects into manageable portions, takes satisfaction in completing intermediate goals, and stops torturing herself with blame and anger about her condition.

Know about these psychological stages and anticipate them. Remember to look back at this section when you feel you're the only one going through this difficult time. You're not. It's normal. This too shall pass. The fact is, when this is over, you're most likely to be happier than you were before you left your last job.

And no matter what, even when you are in the depths of despair, keep sending out new contacts and applications!

I learned this Japanese proverb from my friend Patrick Combs, a motivational speaker and artist: **Fall down seven times. Stand up eight.**

16 Cover Letters: Don't Write One Until You Read Chapter 15

Cover Letters Are Routing Slips

Cover letters serve as routing slips for your resume. Their primary purpose is to get your resume in front of a real live human being and to motivate that human to read further. The more you concentrate on this function, the "routing slip" function, the more successful your cover letters will be. Most cover letters now are in fact just emails, although managers and executives would be well advised to provide a more formal letter as well.

Do not put critical information in only your covering email or cover letter. All critical and substantive points belong in your resume. Your email or letter may be separated from the resume before the ultimate decision-maker gets your documents. This is yet another reason the profile resume is so powerful—your skills and abilities are on the document that counts, not the routing slip.

To control the routing of your resume you always want to write to a person, not a title, a department, or a company. As explained in the last chapter, you must use email and phone connections to get the exact name, title, and email address of your contact. If your queries have not been successful, only then should you resort to writing to a title or department, or *several titles and several departments*.

The one exception to the query-first rule is a blind box ad, a posted opening with the identity of the hiring organization shielded from you. These ads do not name the advertising company, so you do not know whom to query. If you are employed, you should be especially wary of these types of announcements anyway. If you are unemployed or everyone at your company knows you are seeking new employment, then you really have nothing to lose by responding. You can always make your resume anonymous if in doubt. Blind box ads have an undeserved bad reputation. Companies have many good reasons for not announcing their hiring plans, ranging from employee relations to competitive issues.

One way to break blind box ads is to profile the company based on whatever information is in the ad. For example, if they say they are a "$10 million rubber recycling plant based in the Midwest seeking a cost-accounting manager," you identify *all* the rubber recycling plants based in the Midwest. Then you call them up one by one and ask for human resources or the CFO, saying, "I heard you were looking for a cost-accounting manager." The worst thing that will happen is that you'll find some *other* rubber recycling plant needing a cost-accounting manager.

By the way, any time you don't have enough to do in your job search, sit down and start searching company web sites, picking out *any and all email addresses*. Then, email them *all* this query: "I heard you were looking for a [whatever you are]. Who would I talk to about that?" You'll have interviews by the end of the day.

Since I believe you should always tell the truth, right before you hit "send" on that email, say out loud, "XYZ Corp is looking for a cost-accounting manager" (or whatever you are). When you say this, you will also hear it, so your email saying that you heard they were looking for a cost-accounting manager is suddenly true. If they ask you about it later, you can also truthfully say, "I overheard it in my neighborhood." Just kidding.

Of course you should apply via the instructions on the organization's web site or as directed by any posted announcement that you may find, but you *also email your letter and resume to any humans you can identify within the organization*. You don't have to be overly clever about this. Your email can be this simple: "As I understand it, your company is looking for a cost-accounting manager for the Indianapolis rubber recycling unit. I've attached my resume for consideration for that position. Let me know how best to follow up on this."

Having your application read by software and filed for "future consideration" with the human resources department is about as useful as having it sucked into a black hole. Humans count. Databases don't. Don't be fooled by seemingly personal responses generated by software.

The number-one way to get around being filtered by the software is to write to a human being directly, and to identify your mailing as "solicited" or "referred." In your very first paragraph, cite your prior contact or your personal referral source. Few people will thoughtlessly and automatically send your material into the data vacuum, if you have a connection with them. If you can't come up with any other line, use this one: "Donald Asher recommended that I write to you directly. I'm interested in positions in . . . " It doesn't matter if they have no idea who Donald Asher is.

Because of viruses, spam, and phishing, most people will not open an attachment from someone they do not know. On the other hand, attachments are needed so your initial contact can forward your documents to someone else. So it's a good idea to attach the resume *and* include it in the email itself. As mentioned earlier, the standard formats for submitting resumes as attachments are MS Word (.doc or .docx) or Adobe (.pdf). You can lock Adobe files so they cannot be modified if you have any concerns about what will happen to your information. Do know that once the company's software "reads" your resume, they'll have it unlocked anyway. If you write a formal cover letter, *place it in the same file as the resume*. Do not send two or three attachments, or two or three versions, or a picture, or an unsolicited work sample, or anything else as this is just a hassle for the person receiving your application.

Make your heading of the email a little more formal than most. False familiarity, common in email etiquette, is not really appropriate for this type of application. Here are some introductory paragraphs demonstrating these techniques:

Marti Jacobs
Vice President, Operations

Dear Ms. Jacobs:

I was discussing Hyatt operations with Joseph DiMarco, and he suggested that you might be interested in someone with my background. My expertise is IT for resort and hospitality businesses. In the interest of discussing employment opportunities with you, I have attached my resume for your review. The same document also appears at the bottom of this email, for your convenience.

———————

Madison Snyder
Hotel General Manager

Dear Ms. Snyder,

We met a few weeks ago in Chicago at the Ritz Carlton while Nick McRobie was giving a demonstration of Acom software packages. Ever since our conversation about your aggressive projects to retool for the next generation of business traveler, I have been thinking about discussing employment opportunities with you. Toward that end, I have attached my resume for your review. The same document also appears at the bottom of this email, for your convenience.

———————

Robert S. van den Burgh
Director of European Sales

Dear Mr. van den Burgh:

I was discussing my job search with Lars Lundgren recently, and he mentioned you quite favorably. I'm not sure you'll remember me, but we met several years ago in New York. He gave me your current contact information, and suggested that I contact you directly. Since I saw you last . . .

———————

The same technique works with headhunters. If you are a personal referral, your resume will be handled differently than an unsolicited contact.

Dear Ms. Taylor,

I got your name from a professional acquaintance, Mr. Dale Show, director of human resources for Majorfees Group. He said you often have clients who would be interested in someone with my background. Accordingly, I am sending my resume for your review.

If you are responding to a posted opening, cite the job title in your subject line. If there is a job code, do likewise. Companies use these codes to route resumes and track responses, so make it easy for them. Then, repeat the title and code in the text of your email. This makes for idiot-proof routing. Here's an example:

> **From: Tony Bonetti <tonyb@direct.net>**
> **Date: August 3, 2010**
> **To: Clyde A. Watkins <c.a.w.@hr.asiapacific.com>**
> **Subject: Staff Accountant, ACC-27-CB**
>
> Attn: Mr. Clyde Anthony Watkins, Management Recruiter, Human Resources, Eastern Region
> Re: Staff Accountant, ACC-27-CB
>
> Dear Mr. Watkins,
>
> I was recently alerted to your posting by a colleague . . .

Be aware that people mentioned in a posted opening may be fictitious. You are directed to apply to "Susan Scott" but there is no Susan Scott. Some companies use this technique to screen and route contacts, trace advertising effectiveness, etc. So be sure you don't pretend to know Susan Scott.

Also, when you are writing to people in the organization who are not specified in the posted opening, mentioning the job code reveals that you saw the posted opening and that you are now doing something above and beyond what was recommended. In this case, leave out the code. Some version of "As I understand it, your company is looking for a cost-accounting manager for the Indianapolis rubber recycling unit," would be the best approach.

When you are submitting a solicited response, make it overwhelmingly obvious in both the subject line and the first few lines of the email itself.

> Subject: My resume, as you requested
>
> Dear Mr. Witherspoon:
>
> Here is my resume, as you requested in our phone conversation yesterday. I will call you by tomorrow afternoon to answer any preliminary questions you may have. In any case, I look forward to meeting with you on Thursday at nine o'clock. Meanwhile, I hope you are feeling better. I had a similar travel experience recently in Nigeria, but we can talk about that when we meet.

Short emails are usually appropriate for referral contacts as well:

> Dear Charles,
>
> As you requested, I have attached my resume for you to forward to potentially interested parties in Hong Kong. I appreciate your assistance, and I'll call you next week to follow up and see if any of your contacts might have potential.

When to Snail Mail

If a company asks for an application by postal mail, then of course you should comply with that request. If you go to any meetings in person, of course you should have paper copies of all your documents. Otherwise, however, sending a paper resume is a decision requiring some consideration.

On the one hand it is disruptive (in the good sense). People don't receive very many paper resumes anymore. They're physical, and harder to get rid of than hitting that "delete" button. They might hang around on someone's desk for an indefinite period of time. If your letter and resume appear attractive on the printed page, then you're exhibiting mastery of a skill that is increasingly rare: the ability to handle formal business correspondence.

On the other hand, if you are over forty, they may think you are a techie dinosaur. They may think you are sending resumes in the mail because you last read a career book in 1986. They may think you are the opposite of hip, savvy, and *au courant*. They may imagine that you are still looking in some supply closet for typing paper or, even worse, carbon paper.

So if you are over forty or so, I'd think twice about sending a paper resume unless it is requested. If you are younger than that, perhaps you *should* send a paper letter and resume to show you know old school business style. In either case, if you do send a paper resume, my recommendation is that you apply online and make contact with people via email at the same time. And put this line at the bottom of your paper letter and resume: "If you would like an e-version of this document, I'd be happy to provide one. Just email me at john.d.jobseeker@careermail.com."

Executive resume paper is a little heavier than regular (usually 24 lb. weight). White or off white only! Weird paper is almost never a good idea. If your paper has a watermark, make sure each page is printed right-side up. The proper protocol is to staple your resume together, if it is more than one page, and paperclip the cover letter to the resume. I prefer gold-colored paperclips as a nice detail. Consider mailing it in a 9 x 12 envelope so it arrives crisp and unfolded. Remember that in the United States large flats require extra postage even when they weigh less than one ounce.

Cover Letters that Sell Resumes

If your communiqué is going to someone who is not obligated to read your resume, you may need a more traditional cover letter, a sales pitch for you and your resume. These full-bodied cover letters have three functional parts:

- Introduction

- Rationale, or "pitch"

- Call to action

In your introduction, you say why you are writing. Specify the job or functional area in which you are interested and, of course, drop any names or referral sources right away. This can repeat lines in your email; that's fine. Some examples of introductory paragraphs are in the sections above.

Remember to lower the ante. Mention that you would like to "discuss possibilities," or "explore the potential for mutual interest." Do not say anything like "I'll be the best account executive you ever had on your team!"

In the main body of your letter, *you try to set yourself apart from other applicants.* You try to impress your reader with your accomplishments and talents. You can give a logical rationale for your candidacy or some type of sales pitch for yourself based on the quality of your experience and accomplishments.

If possible, relate your strengths to the requirements of the position. Be sure to gloss over or omit reference to any weaknesses. For example, if the ad specifies "college graduates only" and you have no degree, focus on your skills, accomplishments, aggressive sales approach, whatever, but do not mention education at all. The cover letter is no place for excuses or negative points.

On the other hand, you can anticipate your competition, and attack them. "You may have many applicants with more years of sales experience, but take a close look at what I've accomplished. More experience can't beat the type of dedication that I bring to every assignment." Don't be arrogant or dismissive, but doubt-bombing your competition is an edgy strategy.

Be cautious of boasting that you know a lot about your potential employer's business, and avoid statements like "I know I would be a valuable asset to your business." If you have not interviewed for the position yet, that's a bit presumptuous. We will look at some successful examples in a moment.

You do not have to mention why you are leaving your current employer, but if you do, it should be stated in a way that bolsters your candidacy: "My future certainly would be secure with my current employer, but I am not just interested in security. To be honest with you, they do not have any major new projects planned for my business unit, and I would like a new challenge."

In the "call to action" you tell the reader what you want to happen next. Most cover letters, even from very savvy business leaders, lack a definitive call to action. This is the biggest mistake you could make. You must tell the reader what to do next, or suffer the consequences—usually they hit the delete button or forward you to the black hole.

The most effective call-to-action technique is that of telling your reader you will be calling soon, and soon means very soon. Your contacts will read your resume with greater interest and try to remember your name, *all subconsciously*, because they know you'll be calling. Your call is going to have maximum impact during the first twenty-four hours after your communiqué is read. You also will have more impact if you can say precisely when you will call. Here's an example:

"I will call tomorrow morning at ten o'clock to follow up on this email. You can count on me to be prompt. I look forward to answering any questions you may have about my resume or background. If tomorrow is not convenient, I'll understand, and of course you can reach me anytime via email or phone."

If you're too shy to call, tell them you'll check in with them by email to see if they have any questions.

"I will check in with you via email this afternoon to see if you have any questions about my resume or background. Of course you can reach me anytime via email or phone."

Needless to say, if you say you will contact them and you do not, your candidacy is much worse off than if you do not make such a promise in the first place. If you are someone who can't be sure to place a call precisely at 9:59:60 A.M., for example, then give yourself a larger window, "tomorrow before noon," or "by the middle of the week."

An acceptable option when you don't have reliable contact information is simply to ask them to contact you. "Please give me a call to discuss this further, or email me with any questions you might have. I look forward to our conversation."

Be aware of what you're asking for: an exploratory conversation, not an interview and certainly not a job. In fact, try not to use the word "interview" at all. Use these types of wording: "have a conversation," or "answer any questions you may have," or "explore potential for mutual interest," or "see if there is synergy between my background and the challenges your department will face in the near future." When there is no opening, it is usually a good idea to acknowledge this. "I am not applying for a particular position at this time; I am just interested in discussing possibilities. I'll be calling you later today to see if we can arrange a brief get together at your convenience." Promise to take "only a moment" out of the day; if you tell someone you will take only five minutes of her time, that sounds like forever to her. In fact, you may say, "I promise to be respectful of your time, and it will only take a moment to establish whether there's potential for a fit."

Key words to drop into any cover letter are *fit* and *mutual interest.* When you manage your career right, you will be interviewing your contact companies just as closely as they will be interviewing you. The more you realize and act on this, the more respect you will get from your interviewers, and the better "fit" and greater "mutual interest" you will find.

Samples

In all of the following samples, look for the three key functional parts of a cover letter that sells:

- Introduction

- Rationale, or "pitch"

- Call to action

I prefer a cover letter that makes an argument, that in some way gives a rationale for your candidacy. The following letter had a phenomenal response rate for my candidate, even though she did not call and ask for interviews. The reason for her success was the outstanding rationale, which set her apart from the thousands of other, virtually identical candidates.

Dear Hiring Partner:

I am interested in opportunities to serve your firm as law clerk or extern this summer. I have several things to offer that may be of interest to you:

1. My high grades demonstrate my abilities and my desire to perform on your behalf. I have skills in research, writing, and case control. I take my assignments very seriously.

2. Although I am a first-year student, I already have paralegal and legal editing experience. I can be productive without any initial "break in" period.

3. I speak conversational Japanese. If you do any work with native speakers of Japanese, I could be of benefit. Also, I know Japanese business protocol, which is just as important as the actual language.

I am interested in an opportunity to work closely with talented attorneys. I can offer detailed legal skills in support of their activities, accuracy, and a knowledge of my own limitations.

Please call me at your convenience to discuss this further, or email instructions how best to contact you or your designated representative. It would be a pleasure and an honor to be associated with your firm this summer.

Respectfully submitted,

A. Winning Candidate

The following is a style favored by fast-track professionals. It will work with any background with easily quantified, bottom-line accomplishments. The main body of the letter is a big pitch for the candidate; it sells the reader on the candidate's expertise. This particular letter targets a search firm but could easily be modified to target the head of sales for a company.

Dear Ms. Saaban:

I got your name from a friend of mine in human resources, Cindy Ewing, at CYSCO. She said you were the "go to" person for national sales opportunities. I have over 15 years of increasing responsibility as a sales rep and sales manager in the food-service industry. If you have any clients seeking someone with this type of background, perhaps you will be interested in these accomplishments:

- Increased volume by 217 percent for an established company. This was the result of a revitalization of sales efforts. No gimmicks—just hard, smart work.

- Introduced new product to 30,000 pounds in sales in first 90 days, more than 15 times our original target!

- Established sales programs for a new company resulting in 15,000 cases sold in first eight months.

- Earned National Salesman of the Year award in second year with McCormick & Company.

- Trained in sales and marketing with Proctor & Gamble.

I hope you will agree that the above shows a top performer. For additional detail, I have attached my resume for your review. You will see that I have management skills, endurance, and a desire for continued career challenge.

My current company is very happy with my performance, but it has gone through two mergers in the last six months. My position certainly seems to be secure, but I feel it is time for a wise man to consider his options.

If you have anything of interest to discuss, call me at your earliest convenience. I look forward to our conversation.

Sincerely,

A. Strong Candidate

Whenever you write to a headhunter, demonstrate that you understand how the search business works. Ask for a referral to a client, not a lead on a job. Remember that you are in fact the commodity in this equation. Use lines like this: "perhaps your timely introduction could be of benefit to all concerned" or "I should think that any of your clients who are in need of reducing their lead time from R&D to full commercialization would be interested in my accomplishments in this area."

Also, whenever writing to a contingency headhunter, consider putting this line in the letter: "Of course it is understood that you will not forward my material to any employer without discussing the specific opportunity with me first." Otherwise, you may find your resume everywhere, like so much confetti falling over a Manhattan parade.

Although most employment agencies welcome calls and visits from candidates, true headhunters do not. There's no need to call headhunters unless you have a personal connection of some kind. If they have a requisition that's right for you, they'll call. If not, they can't do anything for you.

Broadcast letters can also be used by recent college graduates, or currently enrolled students who are trying to get internships to gain exposure and experience. It helps to have a fairly well-defined employment target, and it really helps if you'll dress well and drop these off in person and follow up with a phone call.

Dear (Mr. or Ms. or Dr. Whatever):

I am a recent graduate of the University of Arkansas's five-year bachelor's program in architecture, which in my case included one year of study abroad at l'Ecole d'Architecture et de l'Urbanisme in Versailles. I am seeking additional experience as a post-baccalaureate intern in your office, prior to returning to complete the master's degree and seeking professional licensure.

It is my desire to contribute in any capacity with a prominent firm. It is not particularly important to me whether there is a stipend or income. Rather, I am eager to work with some talented designers, and participate in the profession of architecture. You will see that I have a solid base of skills to contribute. I have expertise with all the latest drafting and design software (see resume), I have done some very detailed modeling, and my freehand drawing and rendering skills are sufficient to make immediate contributions to client presentations or projects. I am serious about my career, and I am sure you will find my skills and my professionalism are in line with your high standards.

I am seeking to intern with a firm that will offer me ongoing challenge and opportunity. My resume details some of my technical skills, but you cannot tell whether you will be interested in having me assist your staff until you see my portfolio. I think you will find the work of interest, and it will only take a moment to review the portfolio with you.

In order to see if we have a mutual interest, I will be calling you tomorrow before noon. You can count on me to follow through exactly. It would be my pleasure to be available for a brief meeting at your convenience.

Respectfully,

A. Fine Candidate

Here's another model, very different in tone, but also proven effective:

Dear (Mr., Ms., Dr. Whatever):

Before any of us know it, it will be summer, and no doubt your company will want to have some talented interns around to do needed administrative, organizational, and analytical work, to produce special projects that permanent staff don't have time to pursue, and to provide a pool of talent from which to pick promising new hires later.

I'd love to be one of those interns. As a student, I'm gaining leadership and business skills but, more importantly, especially for your business, I already have a very solid background in most office functions. My skills do include an ability to communicate well with both technical and nontechnical staff, and the ability to support mission-critical assignments, and successful experience with diverse, multicultural teams.

Since my interest is to transition to a marketing or product/brand management role upon completing my undergraduate degree, it is critical for me to get a marketing internship this summer. I am hoping that you will see my quantitative skills, my work ethic and strong sense of personal discipline, and my enthusiasm as assets of potential value to you.

I am available 24/7 for travel or assignment wherever you may want me this coming summer. My recommendations are quite favorable (very strong).

Please let me know this: When do you select your summer interns? Who is your internship recruiter, and what is her/his email address? I'd very much appreciate your guidance, and will follow through exactly as you advise me. Here's the best way to reach me: cedawinner@topdrawer.edu.

Thank you very much.

Sincerely,

I. Wanna Getgoing

When applying for a specific opening, you can tailor your entire presentation to keys in the announcement or advertisement. Do make a list of words that you will want to weave into your letter and/or revised resume, but do not use a simplistic, point-by-point presentation that follows the criteria in order from the ad. Instead, read the announcement carefully and see what hints and subtleties you should address. There will be many, many candidates who have the minimum qualifications. You want to be the candidate who answers the employer's unstated but implied concerns.

Develop a prose presentation of your strengths relative to the needs of your target. The bigger the job, the longer your letter can be. The following letter won an interview at odds in excess of one hundred to one, even though my candidate was in Kansas and the targeted reader was a Los Angeles-based personnel consulting firm acting as a screen for the City of Irvine, California.

Dear Mr. Donaldson:

I was interested to come across your advertisement in jobBANK for manager of cultural affairs for the City of Irvine, California. I have been seeking an opportunity such as this, and I think you will find that I might fit your job description. I have attached my resume for your review, along with the background information form you requested in the link from jobBANK.

My background is in city planning and arts administration, which has proved to be an extremely effective combination. I believe my skills, abilities, and accomplishments are represented, albeit briefly, on the attached materials.

In checking my background you will find that I have succeeded in two different but equally important areas: providing effective leadership, direction, and management—and making the arts fun and participatory for a wide range of constituents, from public school students to major benefactors. It is difficult to show "feel good" accomplishments, but you will note that throughout my career I have been able to marshal the support, cooperation, and enthusiasm of an incredibly diverse set of peers and colleagues.

I feel that I have been instrumental in generating long-term benefit for the organizations which I have served, and that benefit can best be summarized as (1) increased financial support, and (2) increased public support, and (3) increased organizational efficiency.

I already have good friends in Southern California, and relocation to the area would be welcome. This position is of great interest to me. I think that your client, the City of Irvine, might be interested in my candidacy as well. Perhaps your introduction would be beneficial to all concerned. Regardless of the outcome, I promise to represent myself, and you, with professionalism.

Thank you for your attention to these materials, and I'll be calling you very soon to see if you have any questions and to discuss your selection process.

Yours sincerely,

A. Fantastic Candidate

The following two pages show cover letters appropriately laid out in a conservative, business-letter format. The first is a targeted application for a management candidate; the second is a broadcast letter for a recent college graduate. Note the strong impression conveyed of the candidates' personalities and work philosophies.

Tara Lynn Johnson

Personal email: tarlynnn@earth.net
Office phone/voicemail: (212) 555-2620
Cell/voicemail/text: (845) 555-3134

White Street, Apt. 5B
New York, New York 10013

October 18, 2010

Attn: **Human Resources**, Department DK
Re: Position for **Collection Manager**, www.WSJ-online.com/updatelist, 10/16/2010
Last Remaining Brokerage, Inc.
Tower Office 4186, 2 Heritage Building
38 Broad Street
New York, New York 10048

Dear Placement Specialist:

I was very interested to see your posting for a collections manager. I have long been interested in your company, and this is a position in which I believe I could excel on your behalf. Per your instructions, I am enclosing my resume for consideration.

As you can see from my resume I have advanced accounting and collections experience for a financial services company. My experience spans multistate collection of receivables ranging from small amounts up to $1 million, collecting from corporate, individual, partnership, trust, and other fiduciary entities. My authority includes direct negotiation and settlement of receivables, and I work with the company's special counsel for collections on cases as warranted. My greatest collection success, however, has been more organizational in nature: (1) training and motivating collections staff, and (2) making contributions to policy and procedure that have drastically reduced our need to pursue overdue receivables in the first place.

Other strengths include (1) management of accounting staff, (2) design of reporting formats, (3) cash management and cash flow control, (4) operations analysis and contributions to design of IT in association with programming specialists, and (5) management of human resources administration. These skills may not apply directly to your position, but my experience in these areas will certainly contribute to my ability to perform.

My orientation is toward preventing problems at the point of origination, but I can be quite creative, persistent, and articulate in both logical and persuasive argument to achieve collections goals.

I hope my background will warrant an interview to discuss this further. Please call me. My office is not far from yours, and I would be happy to meet with you at your convenience to see if we can establish a mutual interest.

Yours sincerely,

Tara Lynn Johnson
Tara Lynn Johnson

Enclosure: resume
Salary: negotiable
/tj

M. J. "Missie" Knobloch

6484 Williams Street
Omaha, Nebraska 68106

Telephone/Message:
(402) 555-1707

June 10, 2010

Attn: Lisa Dale Horton
Vice President, Human Resources
Carfenterium, Inc.
110 South 19th Street
Omaha, Nebraska 68106

Dear Ms. Horton:

I am interested in having a short, face-to-face talk with you about opportunities in human resources with Carfenterium, Inc. As you can see from the attached, I am a recent college graduate with a strong liberal arts education. My greatest strengths would have to be my oral and written communication skills. I am a self-starter. I applied for and thoroughly enjoyed a year abroad, held several elected offices in school, and started a local chapter of a national sorority. I have all the routine office skills, as well as strong organizational abilities as demonstrated in the internships listed on my resume.

I would be interested in an employee relations, training, or HR generalist position involving direct employee contact. Since there are many ways in which I could serve you, I would like to explore that in a brief, personal meeting.

Even if you don't anticipate any openings, a moment of your time would be appreciated. I'd like to hear what ideas you may have for me, and to learn more about human resources as a career.

Thank you so much for your attention. I'll be calling you shortly to see if we can arrange a time of your convenience to get together.

Respectfully submitted,

Margaret Knobloch

M. J. "Missie" Knobloch

Enclosure: resume

Senior management and executive letters can be two-pages long, but most people should try to get the job done in one page. Just for the record, if you write a two-page letter, the top of the second page should have the name of the person you are writing to, the date, and "page 2 of 2." So if you were writing to Linda Smith on August the 8th, 2010, the second page would begin like this:

Linda Smith

August 8, 2010

Page 2 of 2

Letter continues here.

Customize Your Letters

Anyone at the management level who does not write individual, customized letters is not serious about her job search. Even though you will soon develop a handful of letters that you modify only slightly to use over and over again, each one must be individually prepared and free of errors. If you are not a management candidate, however, there is a shortcut that will work in an emergency. The following letter is generic but somehow compelling. Some of my clients who are not comfortable with writing or with computers have used this letter to great success:

Dear Prospective Employer:

In the interest of exploring employment opportunities with you, I have attached my resume briefly describing my qualifications and credentials.

With my experience and background, I am confident that I can make a meaningful and lasting contribution to my next employer. A quick look at my resume will indicate why. Please call me or email me to explore this further, and to see if we can establish a mutual interest.

Thank you for your attention, and I look forward to our conversation.

Yours sincerely,

A. Basic Jobseeker

It's not art, but it'll definitely do the job.

Salary History and References

Do not respond to requests for salary history in a cover letter or any pre-interview communiqué. If it is requested or even demanded, just put a line at the bottom of your cover letter: "Salary history provided on interview."

Salary history can only be used against you, never for you. If they like your background, they'll call you whether you provide salary history or not. If they don't like you, they won't call you anyway. If they really are not considering any applicants who do not provide salary history, then there are many more qualified applicants for the position than needed, and you're statistically unlikely to be hired. Or, worst of all, they're not actually hiring; they're just doing an unethical salary survey on the cheap.

Salary history is not a simple item anyway. There is taxable compensation, or your "total compensation package." Taxable compensation comes off your W-2 at the end of the year. That's base plus any bonuses. You can report it on an annual or monthly basis, but pick one or the other and don't switch back and forth. Total compensation includes taxable income plus 401-K match plus employer-paid health plus the value of any stock options or grants plus such variable perks as the cost of a company-provided car. There is no universal definition of "total compensation package," so a candidate is free to develop his own.

Here's a conservative version of salary history:

Salary History:

Marathon Radiator Corporation, 2007–present

Current: $56,000 per annum

Beginning: $49,000

Jupiter Fender Forms, 2004–2007

Final: $46,000

Beginning: $42,000

Round Tire Company, 2000–2004

Final: $40,000

Beginning: $36,000

Do not provide references until they are requested. You should ask your references ahead of time for permission to use them, and you should prep them on what is important for them to say if they are contacted. Provide references with a current version of your resume.

Tailor your references to the particular application. For example, if your potential employer seems concerned about your financial skills, your first reference should be able to describe a financial problem you solved or financial project you managed.

The usual number of references to provide is three. Ideally, your references would be your immediate superiors in your last two or three jobs, preferably someone with direct knowledge of your daily job performance, not a distant CEO who was thrilled with your production figures but had no working knowledge of you.

You shouldn't have anything in your resume that you are afraid to show to your old employers. If you are afraid to send your resume to them, then perhaps it is inflated. You might want to tone it down to something you know they will endorse.

Be aware that most recruiters and corporate hiring managers will go around the references you provide to find people you perhaps don't even want them to talk with. That's life.

If you're currently employed and you need a reference other than your boss, ask a discreet colleague at work to vouch for you, or a vendor, supplier, or client of your current company.

Have a stable of references, and rotate them so you don't wear some of them out. You may have a few champions who never tire of singing your praises, but you also may have someone who is happy to say great things about you only once in awhile. The last thing you want is for one of your references to say, "Gosh, hasn't she gotten a job yet?"

It is not unreasonable to have a friend in HR or recruiting to check your references if you have any doubt about what people are saying about you.

A reference listing has the name, current title, email, and current daytime telephone number of your endorser. It is optional to list the full street address. If your reference is comfortable providing it, a cell phone is great. If your connection with the reference is not obvious, then state it in parentheses. Here is a conservative reference listing, to go with the salary history above:

References:

Julie K. Samuelson, Vice President of Operations

Marathon Radiator Corporation

jkm@marathonradiator.com

(610) 555-1934, ext. 2186

Cell: (610) 555-2987

Marty Moscovitz, Chief Engineer

Watson Metal & Stamp

(formerly Project Engineer at Jupiter Fender Forms, and my direct boss there)

mm@watsonmetal.com

(610) 555-2949, ext. 209

Brad Warren, Production Supervisor

Round Tire Company

warren@round.com

(310) 555-9594, ext. 2948

Cell: (310) 555-2575

17 Go for It! This Is Your Life

Switching Jobs Is a Life Skill

The ability to switch jobs successfully is a talent like any other. It is a talent that can be learned by anybody and can be improved with practice and study. If you learn this talent well, then you will almost always love your job. Conversely, you will almost never hate your boss, you will be unlikely to feel that your salary is an insult, and you will seldom wonder "what if . . ." for very long before you do something about it.

In the modern job market, your first obligation is to your own career development. If you do not get promotions on a regular basis, or if your company or business unit is imploding around you, then consider a move. If you are not happy, consider a move. My most ambitious clients tell me they expect a promotion every eighteen to twenty-four months. If they do not see a promotion on the horizon on that time frame, they start the process of switching jobs, either internally or into a new organization.

I am not recommending that you sacrifice the rest of your life for your career. On the contrary, I am recommending that you have whatever kind of career you want to complement your life as a whole. The principles in this book are sound. They will work to facilitate your career direction, whatever it may be. They can be translated into the nonprofit sector, government service, or the creative arts.

Set your sights high, whatever that means for you. Go for it. This is your life. You are the boss.

Index